TruthQuest™ Student Commentaries

Christian to the Core

getting deep in the book of James

Steve Keels and Lawrence Kimbrough

CHRISTIAN TO THE CORE
Getting Deep in the Book of James

Copyright © 2004 by Broadman & Holman Publishers
All rights reserved

Broadman & Holman Publishers
Nashville, Tennessee
broadmanholman.com

ISBN 0-8054-2853-4

Unless otherwise noted, all Scripture quotations are taken from the HOLMAN CHRISTIAN STANDARD BIBLE®, Copyright © 1999, 2000, 2002, 2003 by Holman Bible Publishers. Used by permission. Holman Christian Standard Bible®, Holman CSB®, and HCSB® are federally registered trademarks of Holman Bible Publishers.

Dewey Decimal Classification: 227.91
Subject Heading: Bible. N.T. James—Commentaries

Printed in the United States of America
1 2 3 4 07 06 05 04
EB

You know what?

Some people like to dance around the edges with their faith, pulling it out to play with it on Sundays or dusting it off every fall or spring when their church buddies go off to the mountains to camp and cook hot dogs.

But what do we end up with when we treat our Christianity so lightly—as though it's a shirt we can try on if it happens to go with our outfit, or a new combo meal we might order if we've finally gotten tired of the old #1 with a root beer?

We know. We find ourselves feeling awkward and out of place in God's presence, our prayers sounding stilted and anemic, our worship feeling good as long as the beat is solid, but awfully hard to come by when it's just us and the four walls.

So . . . if you've had it with that kind of Christianity—if you're sick and tired of tripping over your own two feet and approaching the Bible like you're a baby crawling on all fours—you've come to the right book.

One good tour through this dead-on letter from James, and you'll find yourself wanting more than the ordinary. You'll sense the Spirit calling you to break out of the disobedience box. You'll want something deeper. You'll want something more.

You'll be begging God to make you *Christian to the Core*.

Ready to Go?

All right. This book is a *commentary*—a verse-by-verse explanation of what the Bible says and what it means. But it's much more than that. It's a way to deal honestly, regularly, repeatedly with the Word . . . and to let God change you from the inside out.

Real quick, let us give you a few tips and pointers on what to expect and how to make the most of this trip.

1] Pack your Bible. This book won't do you much good unless your Bible's right next to it. We're not going to spoon-feed you by writing out all the verses when you can read them for yourself. Instead, we're going to be commenting on them, helping you think about them and sort things out. So you'll need to know what the Bible says to make any sense of what we say.

2] Read ahead. You don't have to, but it wouldn't be the worst thing in the world if you'd go ahead and read the whole book of James first. It's just five chapters, so it won't take you fifteen minutes to get through it. But it'll be well worth every second. Reading a Bible book straight through really—*really!*—helps you understand it better. Even if you (hopefully) take time to do that, still be sure to read each individual Bible passage again first before you read our commentary notes on it.

3] Look back. One of the most important things to know about the Bible is that it proves itself true. Only God could take dozens of writers, space them over thousands of years, and unite all their writings into one book that is totally consistent the whole way through. It's very important, then, to see what God was doing in all the different books of the Bible. So when you come to a place that asks you to look up a verse somewhere, be sure to do it. You'll get a lot more out of the trip that way.

4] Be on the lookout. We've added several sidebars and other features to keep you from missing anything along the way. Here's what they'll look like. And here's what they'll do for you:

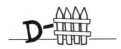

D-FENCE. This will highlight key verses or topics that are foundational to Christian living and thinking. They'll help you be able to defend your faith better, to understand what others believe, and to make sharing Christ a more confident, productive experience.

DEFINITIONS. A lot of words used in the Bible—and the doctrinal terms that come from them—aren't all that easy to understand. Check here to get your fuzzy areas cleared up.

BIBLE REFERENCE. As often as possible, we'll dispatch you to another biblical location where you can see when an idea first shows up in the Scripture, or says something a different way, or gives you a better whole-Bible understanding. (Oh, and also, whenever you see a reference that just lists chapter and verse, like this—12:34, with no Bible book name—that means it's another passage from James).

HISTORY. Part of what makes the Bible hard to interpret is that we don't always know the historical settings it was written in. These little side-notes will give you an idea of things the original Bible audience understood as common knowledge—the same way we understand things in our current culture.

TENSION. Some Bible verses—even after you've read them, and reread them, and read them some more—still don't seem to make any sense. Look for this in-text marker fairly often, where we'll do our best to help you wrestle with—and hopefully start to untangle—the toughest, knottiest passages. Sometimes we'll just have to leave it with a "we don't know for sure," but that's OK. If God's ways were always easy to understand, He wouldn't be much of a God, would He?

TRUTHQUEST QUESTIONS. We've also sprinkled in some room for you to write, to deal with some of the day-to-day implications of what you're reading in James. Be sure not to skip over these or to settle for simple answers. These are important. The Bible is a living book.

5] Use this book as a devotional guide. You can do this fairly easily by going one-by-one to the TruthQuest questions, using the passage where the question is found as your daily Bible reading, then praying or journaling your way through the answers. If nothing else, it'll give you something new to try—different from the usual devotional book or magazine—and it'll hold you for a month or so until God leads you to something else.

Who? What? Where?

James's Facts

- 5 chapters
- 108 verses
- around 2,600 words
- probably written by Jesus' brother
- composed as a letter to the first churches
- contains references to 17 Old Testament books
- perhaps the first NT book written—early as A.D. 48

James's Bio

Two of Jesus' disciples were named James—James the brother of John and James the son of Alphaeus (AL-fee-us). But the James most commonly believed to be the writer of this Bible book is "James, the Lord's brother" (Galatians 1:19). He was perhaps the "James" that Jesus appeared to after His resurrection (1 Corinthians 15:7) and was almost certainly the one who presided as spokesman for the Jerusalem church in Acts 15, where the council decided not to force Gentile (non-Jewish) Christians to behave like Jews in order to be accepted as believers.

In contrast to Paul, who felt called by God to take the gospel to the Gentiles, James was one of those who sensed that his mission in life was to proclaim Christ among his own people, the Jews (Galatians 2:9). He was so devout and committed to this task, however, that some sources tell us he earned the nickname "Camel Knees," because of the crusty calluses he'd gotten from long hours spent kneeling in prayer.

We know for sure that he was murdered for his devotion to Christ, probably as a result of the many Jewish leaders who were converting to Christianity through James's teaching and influence. One historian reported that he was stoned (killed by having rocks thrown at him) by order of the Jewish high priest. Others recount in grisly detail how *before* he was stoned, he was thrown from the temple tower. Amazingly, though—not killed by his fall—he began praying for God to forgive his accusers. Yet they wouldn't relent, and he died at their hands.

James's Book

This book is actually a letter written to the Jewish Christians who had either left or been forced from their homeland. It belongs to the New Testament category called "General Epistles" (or "Letters"), differentiating them from the "Pauline Epistles"—letters written by the Apostle Paul. More than any other New Testament book, James deals primarily with very practical issues, hardly ever ranging into areas that are abstract or hard to understand. But because of his blunt, hard-nosed call to holy living, because of how short his book was, and because some people questioned who wrote it, his letter was ignored by a fair share of early believers.

James's Reasons

Exhorting his readers to live out their Christian beliefs, to sprout legs on their faith, seems to be the main purpose for James's writing. And because he was steeped in an Old Testament outlook, fully immersed in Jewish thought and training—as were many of his readers—he was able to show how obeying Christ was compatible, not contradictory, to the purposes of God throughout human history.

James's Tools

He makes good use of three literary devices that are nice to know in trying to explain your point to someone.

- **SHORT Q AND A:** He peppers his writing with quick, staccato-like questions, followed by punchy answers, like:
  "*Who is wise and understanding among you? He should show his works*" (3:13).
  "*Is anyone among you suffering? He should pray*" (5:13).

- **RHETORICAL QUESTIONS:** These don't require a direct answer because everyone should already know what the answer is:
  "*Didn't God choose the poor in this world to be rich in faith?*" (2:5).
  "*Can a fig tree produce olives . . . or a grapevine produce figs?*" (3:12).

- **FIGURES OF SPEECH:** James uses a lot of analogies to clarify what he meant, to give vivid expression to his teaching:
  "*The doubter is like the surging sea, driven and tossed by the wind*" (1:6).
  "*See how the farmer waits for the precious fruit of the earth and is patient*" (5:7).

James's Big Outline

James skips around quickly from one subject to the next, briefly touching on one theme before jumping to another. So it's not easy to construct the framework of his book in four or five overarching categories, but here goes a stab at making it as concise as possible:

1:1-18   Facing Hard Times
1:19-27 Living by the Book
2:1-13   Treating People the Same
2:14-26 Mixing Faith with Works
3:1-18   Exercising Self-Control
4:1-17   Choosing to Be Different
5:1-6   Being Fair with Money
5:7-12   Waiting on God's Timing
5:13-18 Praying with Faith
5:19-20 Rescuing the Fallen

James's Big Ideas

- **FAITH AND WORKS.** His book is probably best known for making the case that a person's Christian confession should lead logically to a changed, obedient lifestyle.
  "What good is it, my brothers, if someone says he has faith, but does not have works? Can his faith save him?" (2:14).

- **PURE RELIGION.** He distances real Christianity from the in-your-sleep observance of religious ritual, declaring that faith is only complete when it has a practical side.
  "Pure and undefiled religion before our God and Father is this: to look after orphans and widows in their distress and to keep oneself unstained by the world" (1:27).

- **HUMAN EQUALITY.** He comes down hard on those who either let their wealth and position go to their heads, or who treat the poor as if they don't quite measure up.
  "If you show favoritism, you commit sin and are convicted by the law as transgressors" (2:9).

- **THE TONGUE.** James also hits on this point in more than one place, reminding his readers about a little part of their bodies that can do a whole lot of damage.
  "Out of the same mouth come blessing and cursing. My brothers, these things should not be this way" (3:10).

- **WISDOM AND UNDERSTANDING.** He equates true wisdom with the character traits of humility, unselfishness, submission to God's will and way. It is something God offers to us "generously and without criticizing" (1:6), but not so we can "spend it on [our] desires for pleasure" (4:3).
  "The wisdom from above is first pure, then peace-loving, gentle, compliant, full of mercy and good fruits, without favoritism and hypocrisy" (3:17).

- **IMPORTANCE OF CHURCH.** In addition to promoting unity and harmony in the church by treating all people as accepted and welcomed, James also shows our great need for one another—our need to pray for and share our lives with our brothers and sisters.

  "Therefore, confess your sins to one another and pray for one another, so that you may be healed" (5:16).

- **MERCY.** Even with all the tough talk about critical issues that strike us right where we live, stomping on our toes and exposing our hearts, James is careful to say that we are dependent on God's mercy—and honor-bound to be merciful toward others.

  "Mercy triumphs over judgment" (2:13).

James 1

1:1 Hi, It's Me

Family Relations
If you had been Jesus' real-life little brother and you were writing a letter like this, how would you have signed it? Would you have felt like doing at least some subtle name-dropping, just to throw your weight around a little bit? Would you have wanted to make sure everybody knew who they were dealing with here—Jesus' kid brother?

Isn't it just outright unbelievable, then, that James—who truly was the brother of Jesus—would sign his letter as "James, a slave of God and of the Lord Jesus Christ"? Sure, he was actually only Jesus' half-brother, since the two of them didn't have the same biological father. Jesus' father, you remember, was God the Father. But still, James and Jesus had grown up in the same household. They had shared a family name.

So already—with the first sentence of James's letter, we get a look into his humble heart.

Sibling Rivalry
Nowhere in the Bible do we learn exactly how James came to believe that his brother Jesus was the Son of God. We do catch a mention of him as being one of the Lord's flesh-and-blood brothers (Matthew 13:55). We can only assume he joined with the rest of his siblings in their suspicion and contempt of Jesus (John 7:3-5).

SINISTER SIBLINGS.
For a story of real sibling rivalry, go to Genesis 37 and read about what the Old Testament Joseph went through with his bullying brothers.

TWELVE TRIBES.
These were family lines dating back to the sons of Jacob (Genesis 49:28). Every Jewish person was known as coming from one of these families. The "twelve tribes" simply meant all the people of Israel, God's chosen people as a whole.

But it really would have been tough to be Jesus' kid brother, wouldn't it? Can you imagine what it would have been like trying to measure up to His perfect behavior, trying to understand His level of intensity? Jesus was so superior in every way, He would have been an easy target for making fun of and teaming up against.

Talk about sibling rivalry! I mean, his mother treated this kid like He was a King! Who wouldn't be a little jealous?

But somewhere along the line—perhaps before Jesus' left the earth, perhaps after—James became convinced that his big brother was everything He said He was. It must have been hard to repent and admit his mistake, especially if Jesus was already gone. But he did it. James let his big brother come to live in his heart.

DISPERSION.
Also called the diaspora (die-AS-per-uh), this was the scattering of the Jewish people from their central, homeland location in Palestine, caused over time by invasion and persecution. As a result, there were more Jews living outside of Israel in New Testament times than inside.

Dear Friends

James was the leader of the church in Jerusalem, which (as you can imagine) was a pretty important, influential position. By this time there were churches beginning to spring up in cities all over the known world. This expansion followed a "dispersion" of believing Jews from Israel, who were used by God to take the Christian message to other places and nations. But James still maintained a respected platform, a voice of authority, especially to those who shared his Jewish heritage and who were also believers in Christ.

> Do those who have the most to say usually seem to be the most humble, the ones who are least concerned with the way they look or who they know? Why?
>
> _____
> _____
> _____
> _____
> _____

1:2-4 Character on Trial

Life's Headaches

The first readers of James's letter had been driven from Palestine (basically what we think of as modern-day Israel—the Holy Land). So the trials they faced were pretty severe, like:

- Loneliness
- Grief
- Rejection
- Homesickness
- Social isolation
- Language barriers
- Culture shock

But *your* trials can be just as severe. Check off some of the ones you've experienced:

- Divorced parents
- Ridicule for your faith
- A rebellious brother or sister

BROTHERS.
Jesus made this term an expression of spiritual kinship, bigger than blood relations. In the Old Testament, "brother" could sometimes mean a fellow countryman or political ally, but Christ expressed the fact that those who follow God are in a family relationship with each other (Luke 8:19-21). This term refers to male and female believers.

TRIALS.
These are troubles or pressures that can either be a low-level, dull-ache, general sort of thing or a very severe and specific problem, difficulty, or challenge, not usually caused by us but happening to us.

- Money problems at home
- Death of a close friend or family member
- Some kind of handicap or deformity
- Verbal, physical, or sexual abuse
- School or athletic failure

Or write in the margin another kind of trial you've been facing. There's no doubt you're dealing with some. James doesn't talk about trials as if they're optional for us. In fact, he doesn't even talk about "trial" singular but "trials" plural! They're a part of life. We all experience them.

But what we *don't* all experience is *joy* in the middle of our trials.

Happy? About a Test?

James, of course, is not saying we ought to giggle our way through a funeral, or be ecstatic that our best friend is talking about us behind our back. Anyone who thinks like that doesn't understand what joy really is. The joy we experience from trials and hard times is the joy of "knowing."

Of knowing what?

It's the joy of knowing that this trial is good for us, that God is using this trial to develop something in us we could never have accomplished without facing some kind of tight spot or resistance. It's the joy of knowing that God is in control, actively working with us to increase our faith.

Faith, you see, is not some abstract concept that's unattached from real living. Instead, it's like a muscle that stretches and expands when we use it and exercise it. Trials are the gym where faith is built.

JOY.
It's not a feeling but a sense of confidence and deep pleasure that comes from being in right relation to God, from knowing Him and serving Him.

FAITH INCREASE.
When Jesus' disciples asked Him to "increase [their] faith" (Luke 17:5), He didn't hand them a present or put a bonus in their paycheck. Instead He taught them (verses 7-10) about submitting to their Master, obeying His wishes, remembering Who's in charge. For the believer, faith grows through obedience, practice, and perseverance.

Improving Your Grades

Trials can either make you stronger or shake your faith. They can cause you to either run *toward* God or run *away* from God. The choice is yours. But James's challenge was to let them do what they were intended to do in us: produce "endurance."

Trials really are sort of like a test. The same way an exam gives you an indication of how well you know a particular subject at a certain point in time, trials help you see how strong your faith is. They check you out.

So if you truly have a desire for your faith to grow and thrive, you'll be able to endure your next big trial with a sense of joy and purpose. You'll know—God has promised this—that you'll come out stronger on the other side.

TESTING OUT.
In 2 Corinthians 13:5, the Apostle Paul says we should make it a point to "test" ourselves, to see where our faith is.

Growing Up

Have you ever seen a forty-year-old parent acting like a juvenile at a ball game? How embarrassing. Or do you have any of those guys who keep coming around your school even though they graduated years ago? Instead of maturing and moving on, they cling to their high school glory days and keep hanging around long after they should be up and gone.

Maturity doesn't just happen. It's not an automatic switch that gets turned on at 20 or 25 or 30 years of age. Maturity is a choice. And some people never make it. But James tells us that maturity should be a legitimate goal for us. It doesn't mean we have to become boring and lose our youthful excitement about life. It just means we can move toward being more "complete." Mature believers have learned to appreciate the blessings of God and know how to share their fullness with others.

Verse 4. When James says we can reach a point where we're "mature and complete, lacking nothing," does that mean if we suffer and go through enough stuff, we can one day become perfect? Believe it or not, some Christians have believed this, even though human perfection is obviously impossible. But in each trial, there is perhaps a certain level of maturity God wants to grow in us. Amid the overall process of maturing for a lifetime, we really *can* succeed in receiving the full measure of what God desired to do in us during a particular period of time.

HEATING METALS.
The crucible was a pottery vessel used to heat metals (primarily silver) to a high temperature, which helped refine it and eliminate impurities. Brick and stone furnaces were used for heating many other metals, like iron and copper. Many times the Bible speaks of these hot spots in figurative language, as places of testing and purifying (like in Proverbs 17:3 and Isaiah 48:10).

GOD'S TESTING.
God has always used testing to help His people grow in their faith. He tested Abraham (Genesis 22:1), the children of Israel (Exodus 16:4), the deacons in the early church (1 Timothy 3:10). Look up test, tested, and testing in your concordance, and you'll find a good Bible study waiting to happen.

? How has God used a trial in your life to teach you a lesson?

_____
_____
_____
_____
_____
_____

1:5-8 Praying for Wisdom

The Places Where Wisdom Grows

You probably don't think all that much about your need for wisdom. Oh, maybe you'd like a little dose of it to help you with your homework tonight! But more than likely, you don't wake up in the morning with a deep-down craving for God's wisdom.

But you'll face some choices today, no matter how small and seemingly simple, that will require you to make some judgment calls. When these choices come up, you'll base them on either your own best hunches or on the wisdom God gives you through His Word and through His Spirit's direct guidance.

And down the road—if not already—you'll be faced with some decisions so big, you'll know without looking that you'll need God's wisdom in order to make them.

- Whether or not to go to college
- If so, which one to enroll in
- If not, which direction to take
- Someone to marry
- Which jobs to apply for

The choices will just keep getting bigger and bigger as you get older. But if you've already been in the habit of seeking God's wisdom for the smaller issues of life, you'll find yourself naturally turning to Him and receiving His wise counsel on the more substantial ones.

So when you recognize that you've been given too much change at the drive-thru window, does God's wisdom kick in for you? When there's a racy show or commercial on television and nobody's in the room to

WISDOM.
More than just information and knowledge, wisdom involves a sense of right understanding, moral discernment, spiritual insight, and perspective that leads you toward good, responsible choices and opinions.

SOLOMON.
Surely, the best Bible example of someone asking for wisdom is King Solomon's request in 1 Kings 3. Turn there to see a generous God who gave him more than he asked for (verses 10-14), as well as an immediate example of how Solomon put God's wisdom into practice (verses 16-28).

PROVERBS.
"Wisdom is supreme—so get wisdom. And whatever else you get, get understanding" (Proverbs 4:7). The book of Proverbs is a collection of nothing but wisdom and memorable sayings. Because it's arranged in 31 chapters, many people read one a day each month as an ongoing Bible study plan. Not a bad idea, huh?

know you're watching it, does God's wisdom have a say in your reaction?

A God Who's Quick to Give

There's a lot of info on the Web, a lot of advice from so-called experts, and a lot of research reported and slanted one way or another. But that doesn't make it *wisdom*. Wisdom, according to James, is the special gift of God.

Not only is God full of wisdom on every conceivable problem or question, He is also willing to give it to us "generously" and "without criticizing," without favoritism and without holding back.

This doesn't mean we should expect His wisdom to arrive in the afternoon mail or be boomed from the heavens in a thunderstorm. For starters, the Bible that's hopefully resting there beside you is already a treasure chest of God's wisdom. Surprise: Everything you'll ever need to know in order to live a healthy Christian life is already spelled out for you right there in black and white.

Some of your decisions, though, won't be between right and wrong, but between good and best . . . or between bad and worse. The Bible may not give you a case-specific answer. Yet whether you're opening the Word in pursuit of God's wisdom or needing detailed direction from Him about a certain issue, your approach should be the same: prayer. Not just prayer, but asking "in faith," fully believing that He will lead you to the right passage or make His will and wisdom known to you in some other way . . . at the time He knows is best.

This God of yours, remember, is a generous giver. So when you come to Him for help, you can expect Him to give it. Can you "ask in faith" and believe that?

I Doubt It

But some can't seem to ask in faith. James has a word for them: they're like the waves on the ocean. They're up one minute and down the next. You can't get your arms around them. As soon as you think you know where they stand, they spin around and you can't find them anymore. One minute they're breaking out of the pack, the next they're mingling back into the crowd, hard to distinguish from everything else around them.

Now, obviously there are times when you're not sure what to do in a certain situation. You're leaning one way, but you're still not totally decided. That's normal. That's life. That's not the kind of "doubting" James is talking about.

The ones who are guilty of the verse 6 kind of "doubting" are the ones who aren't so sure they believe verse 5—that God is all-wise, and that His wisdom can really be known. They're not willing to believe that God is generous, that He will truly give "without criticizing." They haven't fully gotten it through their heads that they are forgiven and in right standing before Him. Consequently, He delights in showering wisdom on them so their lives can be a clear demonstration of His power.

FAITH AT SEA.
Whenever we're not faithfully spending time in the Word or being an active part of a church community, we're all susceptible to this seasick feeling of not knowing which way is right and which end is up. Ephesians 4:14 talks about this.

FAITH AND WORKS.
James is the Bible author most noted for making clear this concept: Faith and obedience work hand in hand, for "faith without works is dead" (2:26). We'll talk a lot more about this later.

Double Standard

Jesus said, "Take care how you listen [to His word, to His wisdom]. For whoever has, more will be given to him; and whoever does not have, even what he thinks he has will be taken away from him" (Luke 8:18). That's the way it is with those who doubt they'll hear anything of real value from God: they even lose the ability to use the good sense He's already given them.

Jesus also said, "Every kingdom divided against itself is headed for destruction, and no city or house divided against itself will stand" (Matthew 12:25). When we try to unhinge obedience from Christian faith, we find our feet in two boats going in opposite directions.

Take the example of a Christian girl getting into a dating relationship with an unbeliever, or even a person who claims to be a Christian but who obviously doesn't take his faith very seriously. Her Christian friends do all they can to warn her that she's heading for trouble, that she's letting her heart rule her head, but she won't listen. The Bible itself is very clear about not allowing this (2 Corinthians 6:14), but she falls for the rationalization that has led to many an unhappy break-up or destroyed marriage: "He'll change."

So when God's wisdom and our stubborn wills collide, we end up being an unstable mixture of faith and faithlessness. Pretty soon, this spiritual shakiness spills over into every other activity and relationship in our lives, into "all [our] ways."

> If God's wisdom seems like a hard thing to access, where do you think the breakdown is happening? Why might you be experiencing His silence?

_____
_____
_____
_____
_____

1:9-11 Richer or Poorer?

Role Reversal

If you thought it sounded illogical to say that *joy* should be our first reaction to trouble, wait till you hear how James tells us to feel about being short of cash. Are you ready? Deeply happy, almost prideful.

Now this doesn't mean that being poor is better than being rich. It just means that all believers—yes, all of us—have a rich, eternal future with God. And if we *do* happen to have money, we should rejoice, not because we have it, but because we don't really need it—because we already have everything we need in our relationship with Christ.

ALL WE NEED.
Make it your constant mindset to realize that you already have "everything required for life" through your relationship with Jesus Christ (2 Peter 1:3-4). This is not just a sweet thought—overly spiritual wishful thinking. This is true! He is everything!

Happy Where You Are

There's no doubt that in this world—even in the church, sometimes—being rich is considered way better than being poor. I mean, how do you feel about

FADING FLOWERS.
This analogy that likens us to a "flower of the field" comes from Isaiah 40:6-8 and is repeated in various places throughout the Bible. Only the Word of God will stand forever.

people who can pretty much buy anything they want? You may be miserably jealous of them, but chances are you wouldn't mind changing places with them for a while! Think of the silly TV shows that are based on becoming a millionaire, hitting the jackpot, and having it all. Let's face it: we are stuck on money—even the money we don't have!

Yeah, even those who *don't* have much money often do everything they can to act like they do—by shopping in the right kinds of stores and showing off whatever brand names they've been able to buy. But James is saying that we shouldn't put so much stock in things that have such a short life span. If you're poor, don't worry about it. If you're rich, don't dwell on it. Rich and poor are both on equal ground at the foot of the cross.

And the rich and poor who are members of the church should understand this better than anybody.

Wither Away

Picture a beautiful, springtime lawn—thick, lush, and green—soft and luxurious under your bare feet on an April morning. Then fast-forward to late August after a blistering, hot summer has burned up the grass at the roots. Life has turned to death in a matter of months. Even the leaves have begun losing their color, many of them snapping off and falling to the ground. All is brown, decaying, and dying.

Now imagine that the green grass of April represents the people who were alive and well not too long ago but who are now dead and gone . . . like a brittle August lawn. That's what happens, year in and year out. In your town or city alone, many people have died

BIBLICAL CLIMATE.
The winds coming off the deserts in Bible lands were nice and balmy at times, but more often they would sear the land and dry up the vegetation. Like a blast of heat from an oven, this scorching wind known as the sirocco (shuh-RAH-ko) had the power to wither flowers in a matter of minutes.

in the past year. How many of them did you know personally? Not many? How many will you ever think about again? One or two of them? Maybe?

The Certainty of Death

If you're like most students—or even a lot of grownups—you probably feel like you're invincible. The possibility of death rarely enters your head. But all of us—rich and poor alike—will one day face the unavoidable. Even those who felt like they had the most influence, who expected to leave the biggest footprint on the world, will be replaced by next year's green shoots and sprouts.

That's why, for a Christian, categories like rich and poor shouldn't apply or be aspired to. We should be so aware of our short-term status, and so assured of the strong relationship Jesus has given us, that we no longer want things that won't last.

DATE WITH DEATH.
Perhaps no other verse puts it quite this abruptly, but in about half a breath, Hebrews 9:27 sums up the reality of our future: "It is appointed for people to die once—and after this, judgment." Expect one hundred percent attendance.

> Have you ever been to the funeral of someone who was about your age? How did that affect your understanding of life and death?

BEATITUDES.
From a Latin word meaning "happy." These are statements (like the one in verse 12) that typically begin with the word "blessed" and describe the good things that come to us from being in right relationship with God. The most well-known beatitudes in the Bible are from Jesus' Sermon on the Mount (Matthew 5:1-12).

CROWN OF LIFE.
A head wreath was given as a victor's prize in the ancient Greek games, yet it was subject to decay over time. But God will give us an unfading crown of eternal life. In other places it's referred to as the "crown of glory" (1 Peter 5:4) or the "crown of righteousness" (2 Timothy 4:8).

1:12-15 Trials and Temptations

But Do You Love Him?

In verse 3, James helped us see that trials and tough times are test days for our faith. Yet they are also tests of our love, as he says in verse 12. Those who stand tall in their trials are not only those who have *faith* in God but also those who *love* Him.

Do you want to love Him more? Then let Him show you how to face a difficult day, month, or year without dissolving into bitterness, whining, and despair. You'll wake up one day with not only a stronger faith in God but a deeper love for Him, too.

You can do it. Notice that James doesn't say *if* you pass the test but "*when* you pass the test." And with it will come a crown of life, "promised" to you by a truth-telling God who is there for you all the way . . . and will be there for you to the end.

Trials vs. Temptations

Trials and temptations aren't the same thing. Trials are more of what we think of as a hardship, a problem, a hurdle to get over. Temptations, though, are enticements for us to sin, to do evil.

There are basically two types of temptation. One kind is directly from the Devil, like the temptation Jesus experienced (Matthew 4:1-11). The other kind is the one James describes in verses 13-15, where we pretty much do it to our own selves.

When we treat our sinful desires as if they weren't really all that big of a deal, or when we're not careful to stop our lustful thoughts or our gossipy lips at the first sign that they're taking over, we give the Devil room to lead us even further astray. This is probably most easily seen in a dating relationship that creeps little by little over the borderline until, well . . . you know.

But one thing's for sure: God never tempts anyone. There is no evil in Him, and no desire for Him to bring about evil in our world or in our lives.

Verse 13. If "God is not tempted by evil," then how could Jesus have been tempted by the Devil? Were the Devil's offerings not really tempting to Jesus? To help figure this out, remember that Jesus was both 100 percent divine and 100 percent human. You're right when you say that Jesus the Son of God could not be tempted. But Jesus the son of Mary could be tempted. If not, then He wasn't really a man.

DUALISM.
Some people believe that good and evil are equal forces in the universe, constantly duking it out to see which one will win [dual meaning "two"—dualism]. The Star Wars movies are pretty much based on this theology. But the Bible clearly affirms that "God is not tempted by evil" [1:13]. Evil only exists because God allows it. He is not in danger of being defeated by it.

Anatomy of a Temptation

James's description of temptation works like this: Let's say you have a tendency to be harsh and critical of others. Every time someone in church asks you to think of "the one sin you have the most trouble with," this is yours. You've really tried to deal with it lately, and God has been helping you. But one afternoon while killing some time with your friends, they start talking about what a jerk this one particular person at school is.

Okay. The Holy Spirit starts waving red flags in your conscience, and you know you're teetering on the edge of jumping right in there with them. I mean, you've thought the same thing about this person a hundred times, and you could really get some laughs with some of your biting comments. Here's your chance to

TEMPTATION'S LIMITS.
One really encouraging verse that helps us deal with temptation is 1 Corinthians 10:13, which reminds us that [1] temptation is an experience common to all human beings, [2] the Devil can't force us to comply, and [3] there's always a way out, if we'll look for it.

SIN = DEATH.
The fact that sin leads to death is not just written in the Bible but is evident in every news broadcast, visible in the lives of people you know, and an unavoidable conclusion in most books and movies. Be watching for these modern day images of sin's nasty side-effects. They will help you more clearly explain why God's life is so much better.

see if you can keep quiet when everything inside you is wanting to join the club. But with one conscious decision, you push aside the Spirit's warning and crack a joke at this person's expense.

At this point the floodgates are open. There's no stopping you now. Your comments get worse and worse—and easier to let fly. There's less resistance now. You've let your human nature have room to play, and now it's beating up your good intentions.

> Have you noticed how this slow, little-by-little descent into sin happens in your own life? What are some things you've done to stop sinking when you've felt yourself sliding down?
>
> _____
> _____
> _____
> _____
> _____

1:16-18 What a Good God

Faked Out

The fact that we can lure our own selves into sin is reason enough for James to make this warning in verse 16: "Don't be deceived." We really *can* fake ourselves out. We can trick ourselves into believing that our sin isn't really all that bad (1 John 1:8). We can twist our view of God around until He looks a little more like we want Him to look (Psalm 50:21).

By letting ourselves be driven by our own smarts and feelings rather than our faith in Him and His Word, we shrink God down to manageable size and raise our own esteem out of proportion.

Father of Lights

Everything that's good is a gift from God. Good has no other source than God. Even those who don't believe in Christ but who do nice things (like helping you with your homework) are only able to do good because God has chosen to be good to them.

This is known as God's "common grace," His willful choice to cause "His sun to rise on the evil and the good" (Matthew 5:45). This is His "generous act" of love that lets Christians and non-Christians alike enjoy the taste of a cherry snow cone.

Not only is He good, but He is also *unchangeable*. He is even more certain than the stars, the sun, and the moon He created that continue to appear in the sky—day after day, night after night. He is constant and steady. He casts no shadow because there is no light brighter than He is; nothing can eclipse His glory. As the old childlike prayer goes, "God is *great*, and God is *good*." And let us thank Him for always being who He always says He is ... and who He always will be.

UNCHANGING GOD.
The big word for this is immutability (im-MUTE-ability), meaning that God can't change, can't "mutate." He will never become someone He hasn't already been. This is a vitally important piece of Christian doctrine, because think of how awful and unsettling our lives would be if God could change: He could turn against His people. He could become evil. He could reverse course and repeal His promises. Nobody needs that.

Loved into Life

The contrast is striking. Sin, no matter how cool and attractive it likes to present itself, is nothing more than a disguise for the death that lies behind it. Yet our loving Father, even when His holy standards seem hard and inconvenient, is our one and only doorway to life.

FIRSTFRUITS.
According to the Old Testament law, the Israelites were to bring a portion of their first harvest —the best of the best— to present to God as an offering of gratitude (Numbers 15:17-21). This term is used in many later Bible passages to describe what God's people are like in His eyes—the most valuable of all His creation.

Sin kills, but God has given us "birth." Sin is a lie, but God's Word is the "message of truth."

And so while it's true that we are all born lost and defenseless, without a shred of goodness to our name, the Lord "by His own choice" has given us hope in His Son, Jesus Christ. The gift of salvation is not a constitutional right, not something we deserve or are entitled to receive. It's the loving choice of a merciful Father.

Sin stripped us of our value, but God has redeemed and elevated our value above everything else He created—even angels and snow-capped mountains and cute, cuddly kitty cats. In Him we have ultimate value. We are as sweet to Him as the first tomato out of the garden in the summer. Through the love of the Father of lights, we have the gift of life.

> **?** What are some of the good gifts God has given you?
> _____
> _____
> _____
> _____
> _____
> _____

1:19-21 The Answer to Evil

Listen Up

James knew that God's people were more than just valuable to themselves. They also were valuable to God. They were living examples of His character, daily reminders to others of the transforming power of Christ.

Remember that Christianity was just getting started in the early to middle part of the first century. Christians were being watched like hawks, suspected of being just another kooky new religious cult. If they were to have any impact for Christ in the places where they lived, there had to be a noticeable difference in their lives.

So let's start small, James seems to say . . . with everyday things, like . . .

Keep Quiet

Do you know somebody who just talks all the time? Have you ever been in a class or Bible study where one or two people totally dominate the discussion? They think what they have to say is so much more important than anyone else's ideas. Well, how do you feel about them? Does it make you want to be as smart and outgoing as they are? Or does it just make you wish they'd put a sock in it?

There is something calm, peaceful, and strangely powerful about people of few words. They don't feel like they always have to know everything. They don't seem overly concerned about making (or faking) a good impression. They are controlled and deliberate. The things they say are genuine and thought out. Their

THE TONGUE.
James deals pretty extensively with the need to control our speech and with the impact our words can have for either good or evil. This was already a clear theme from the Old Testament (Proverbs 10:19), and we'll see even more of it in chapter 3.

words *weigh* something. Wasn't that the way Jesus was? Isn't that the way we should be?

Calm Down

Here's another one: our temper. When someone in authority over you—a parent, a principal, a coach, a deacon at church—requires something of you or disciplines you in some way, what is your first response? Is it acceptance and obedience? Or is it anger? What do you do when you feel the skin on the back of your neck flash and burn?

Was anger a habitual response of Jesus? You see it flare in Him a few times, when needing to make sure His disciples were focused on their mission or when confronting hypocrisy and greed. But did Jesus ever get angry just because He wasn't getting His way or getting enough sleep? Never. Selfish anger "does not accomplish" a very persuasive witness of "God's righteousness."

Straighten Up

You may feel totally helpless when it comes to controlling your tongue. You may have a hard time keeping from cussing, for example. You may be one of those whose language and topics of conversation are hardly less bathroomlike than any other potty mouth at your school. How do you overcome a problem like that?

James says you do it first by recognizing that "moral filth" and "evil excess" have truly invaded your thoughts. (That's why they're now coming out of your mouth.) And next, you make a promise to take seriously the "implanted word" of the Bible and the Holy

THE WORD.
We tend to interchange "the Word" and "the Bible" as though they're one and the same thing. And they are ... sort of. But the "word"—even now, but especially at James's point in history, when the New Testament wasn't even formed yet—doesn't really mean the words on a Bible page. The "word" is the authority of God that inspires and animates the Scriptures. The "word" is God's truth, revealed to us in words we can understand ... in the Bible.

Spirit who lives inside you. You no longer just *read* it—you "receive" it—letting the Scriptures be an everyday assignment, not just a nice, Sunday saying.

> **?** When do you find it the hardest to control your tongue? In what situations do you most often say things without thinking?

1:22-25 Both Eyes on the Word

I Don't Think So

Here's what happens in a believer's life if the Bible is just a book to read, rather than a word to follow.

Every time we open the Bible, we're seeing God, ourselves, and our world the way it really is. Our eyes and our experience may tell us differently, but what God says in the Bible is the only honest truth.

Sometimes, though, the Bible seems like it lives in another world. It may sound right and fine while we're reading it, but out in the middle of an average school day, some of that stuff just doesn't seem all that relevant.

When we "deceive ourselves" enough to believe that, however, a disconnect starts to happen in our lives. We know what the Bible says, but we're not all

MIRRORS.
In Bible times, mirrors were made of polished metal. It wasn't until the late Roman period—perhaps the time of James's writing—that glass mirrors became available. Up until then, people would more likely think of a mirror the way Paul described it in 1 Corinthians 13:12—a way of seeing "indistinctly."

that keen on obeying it. So we sort of become two people: our spiritual side believes things our physical side doesn't want to live out. The result is the "indecisive man" from verse 8, "unstable in all his ways."

All for One

The opposite happens, though, when the Bible becomes more than words on a page—when it becomes reality in action. Like we said, those who see God's Word as a law of *restriction* rather than a "law of freedom," those who *piddle around* with it rather than "persevering" in it, are assured of feeling the curse of the "forgetful hearer." Phoniness. Confusion. Imbalance.

But those who are both "hearers" and "doers" are "blessed" as a result. They enjoy the sweet relief of being the same person in private they profess to be in public. Their behavior allows them to feel comfortable staying in God's presence, not distant and ashamed or jumping in and out of His will.

LAW.
The Jewish readers of this letter would have certainly understood the "law" to be the Ten Commandments and the written Scriptures. God had always intended this to be a "law of freedom"—freedom from unhappiness, from self-inflicted turmoil and consequences. Many, however, found the law confining, a burden. Not until they'd heard the teachings of Christ did they understand that even do's and don'ts can be liberating.

FREEDOM.
One of the great truths of the gospel is that Christ has set us free—free from empty form and ritual (Galatians 2:19-21) and free from slavery to sin (Romans 6:16-18).

> How can we help each other remember what God wants us to see in His Word, instead of merely looking at it, walking away, and forgetting it?

_____
_____
_____
_____
_____
_____
_____

1:26-27 Christianity, Pure and Simple

Tongue Depressor

You wonder why James seems so worried about the words we say. I mean, shouldn't he be spending more time coming down on the murderers and adulterers? Surely there's more harm done by thieves and robbers than by cussers and gossipers!

But here's the deal: As Jesus said, "The mouth speaks from the overflow of the heart" (Matthew 12:34). Long before most people work their way up to the more notorious sins (or down, you might say), the people around them can tell which way they're going by the words they speak. You can hear it in their tone of voice. You can spot it in their sharp replies and quick tempers.

Deception starts in a person's heart, then it leaks out through his vocabulary. When our mouths are starting to get us into trouble, it's time to take a serious look at what's rotten on the inside.

Keep It Up

"Pure and undefiled religion." That's what both James's world and our world have long needed to see from Christians. They need to see people who are genuine and authentic. People who take their faith seriously even when it costs them. People who are not only known by the bad things they *don't* do but by the good things they're actively *doing*.

You can see the difference on the outside. You can measure it by the number of people you're serving and helping. You can tell it by the way you do things for

DEFILEMENT.
Cleanness was a big part of Israel's moral and spiritual life. Certain diseases or behaviors could make a person defiled and unclean, requiring a ritual of purification before he or she could function again in society and be part of public worship. James's readers knew how important it was to be "undefiled" [verse 27].

WIDOWS AND ORPHANS.
These were considered the most helpless members of society. In a culture so centered around the family, the ones who had no father or husband became social misfits with no one to provide for them or to represent their interests in the courts. But God the Father has always had a heart for the helpless, and the Bible frequently teaches us to help those who have been stripped of normal assistance.

people you don't even like all that much. You can enjoy it by seeing the smiles and gratitude of the people God blesses through you.

Keep Away

But you can also sense it on the inside. You can operate in a world that's punkish and profane, yet keep your heart pure and unpolluted. You can make a difference in people's lives who don't look anything like Christians, yet resist the temptation to follow around acting just like them.

You'll look different when you do this. But "different" is one of the telltale signs of a Christian, just like it was of Christ. Some people were never quite sure how to take Him. But they knew without a doubt that there was something intriguing, astonishing, different about Him. The world should be able to say the same of us.

> **?** What keeps you from experiencing "pure and undefiled religion"? Lack of time? Fear? Unconcern for other's needs? Too much concern for your own reputation? What?
>
> _____
> _____
> _____
> _____
> _____
> _____

James 2

2:1-4 Playing Favorites

Picking and Choosing

James talks about "favoritism" in terms of rich and poor, but we know it goes much further than that. We size people up for preferential treatment based on lots of different reasons: how physically attractive some people are, or how popular they are, or what kind of friends they hang around with. In doing this, we slide into a sin that crosses three biblical boundaries:

1) We invalidate our "faith" (verse 1). As James discusses in much greater detail near the end of this chapter, faith is an action verb in the Christian's grammar books. So when we do things that are ungodly, we not only give other people reason to question the sincerity of our faith, we also give the Devil room to make us doubt it ourselves.

2) We trust outward appearances (verse 3). The Bible is one big story after another of God's desire to change our hearts, to make us true on the inside. By basing our acceptance of other people purely on their cute blonde hair or their basketball moves, we deny the fact that the real measure of a person's stature is the kind of character they're growing.

3) We set ourselves up as "judges" (verse 4). The Scripture is quite clear that "judging" other people is God's business, not ours. We are not to "owe anyone

FAVORITISM.
This comes from a word that means "to lift up our face on a person"—which doesn't become a problem until we're partial about who we speak to and associate with.

anything, except to love one another" (Romans 13:8). So we'll save ourselves a lot of needless worry and repentance if we'll simply treat everyone as being worthy of our attention.

Favoritism in Action
You get the feeling from James's story in verses 2-4 that he's not just making up this example in his own head. He had probably seen it with his own two eyes—a rich man coming into church and being treated to smiles and "good-to-see-ya's" and a nice seat down front, while a less showy person is shown the floor.

We've seen it, too—a top-dog athlete who marches into the lunchroom to the tune of turning heads and instant attention. Perhaps besides being a good ball handler, though, this kid is also a bully. He cuts people down without thinking twice. He's foul-mouthed and undisciplined and (everyone knows) he's sleeping with his girlfriend. Because he's so cool and popular, though, there's hardly a person in the room who wouldn't stand a little taller if he noticed them.

But who even looks up from their lukewarm cafeteria lunch when a person walks in who's much less popular, though perhaps much more godly? You could ask yourself a lot of questions like this. For example, do you have an immediate, standard reaction to people of different races and ethnic backgrounds? Are you constantly making fun of the computer nerds or the chess club crowd? Or if you're *one of* the chess club crowd, do you look down on others just because they're not as smart as you are?

James calls this kind of discrimination the result of

CHURCH MEETINGS.
Unlike many religious groups of the first century, which often required long periods of probation before a person was received as a full member, the early Christian church was called to embrace all those who believed on Christ. If Jesus was willing to accept and forgive them—warts and all—it was important for church members to accept them too.

"evil thoughts"—strong words for an offense we usually take rather lightly. We do well to realize, though, how "evil" even our little sins really are.

> **?** What do you make of celebrities—actors, singers, athletes—that you love to see perform, but who are walking examples of scandal and self-centeredness? Do you still admire them?
>
> _____
> _____
> _____
> _____
> _____

PARABLES.
James used object lessons (like the one in verses 2-4) much like Jesus used them in His teaching. These short stories, cut from real life and chock-full of real issues, are a great way to explain hard biblical concepts in ways people can understand. If you keep your spiritual eyes open, you'll be able to spot storylines like these in everyday events and use them to tell others how faith works.

2:5-7 Questions about Favoritism

A Heart for the Poor

This section is made up of three rhetorical questions—(questions James expects us to answer with a "yes")—that give a practical rationale for his teaching on discrimination. The first question deals with God's brand of favoritism.

We know from Scripture, of course, that "there is no favoritism with God" (Romans 2:11). He has no teacher's pets who are allowed to do anything they want and get away with it. But His heart *is moved* toward the poor—not necessarily the ones who are poor economically, but those who are in need of Him and know it, those who come to Him for their supply. We, too, should never be fooled just by the way poor

POVERTY.
Although James indicates that there were pockets of discrimination against the poor, the church as a whole seemed to take its responsibility to the poor seriously. The early church appointed deacons ["servants" or "ministers"] to actively assist the needy [Acts 6:1-6], and Paul mentioned several times how he had raised money from the churches to help the poor.

people appear when side-by-side with the successful. Who knows? They may actually be "rich in faith and heirs of the kingdom." If not, perhaps our kindness to them will help them *become* rich toward God as they learn to "love Him." Wouldn't this be the way God wants us to relate to other people?

Verse 5. If God doesn't want us to show favoritism toward others, then why does He do it Himself? I mean, if it's wrong to show favoritism to the rich, isn't it just as wrong to show favoritism to the poor? Yes. But God alone—unlike us—is in a position to seek glory for Himself. This is not a matter of pride on His part; this is just something He rightly deserves. And because the poor are usually quicker to realize their dependence on Him, God does "choose" people who have little in the way of human advantages as a way of highlighting what He can do. Because no one expects much from them, God's power is the only real explanation for their joy and the things they accomplish.

Who Cares?

Not all the popular people you know are jerks and hypocrites. And not all the "rich" are like the ones included in the examples James gives. But here's a modern-day variation on questions #2 and #3:

"Who's more likely to make time for you if you need help with something? A third-year cheerleader or a third-string tackle? A stuck-on-himself school jock or an all-by-himself classroom joke?"

Yet many of us invest the bulk of our time trying to

get the right people to notice us, trying to catch the eye of those who really couldn't care less about us.

> A whole lot of people out there would love to know they mattered to somebody. How could you go about showing them that they matter to you?

2:8-13 The Standard Sentence

The Golden Rule

Christianity wouldn't be such a hard faith to live if we weren't so stuck on ourselves. We're always fixing up, trying on, working out, or thinking about how we look. But if we could just transfer this obsession we have for ourselves into love for one another, imagine how God could use us to make a real difference in the world!

Sure, this requires an enormous amount of self-sacrifice. But in many ways, it's fairly basic and simple. That's why James (in quoting Jesus) boils down the "royal law" to a simple sentence: "You shall love your neighbor as yourself."

Think about it. By applying this one little phrase to just about every decision you make in your relation-

GOLDEN RULE.
The words "golden rule" don't appear in the Bible. But this "love your neighbor as yourself" principle (verse 8—quoted from Leviticus 19:18) was a uniquely original biblical concept, although forms of it appear (stated differently, in negative fashion) in the teachings of other religions.

TRANSGRESSORS.
Just as progress means "to advance" and regress means "to go back," transgress means "to step beyond or across a boundary." Transgressors are those who dare to go where God's law forbids them to travel.

ships with other people, you can almost always instantly know what you should do. The answer may not be easy to carry out, but it's usually quite easy to understand. This "royal law" is the standard sentence for Christian ethics.

Messing Up Royally

Even with something as "minor-league" in the sin department as "favoritism," the standard "guilty" sentence for this offense still applies. The "lawbreaker" charge stands up just as well against small-time sinners as it does against murderers and fornicators.

That's because there's never a time when our sin is simply the breaking of a single command, nor is it ever a violation of mere words on paper. Every sin is an offense, not against the law but against the Law*giver*.

That's why when we play loose with even a sub-level sin, we're as guilty as those who do things that are far more premeditated. The true foul we commit when we sin is not the specific act we do. It's the way we trample on God's holiness while we're doing it.

Verse 10. Is God being a little too strict here? What ever happened to three-strikes-and-you're-out? Why the zero-tolerance policy when we have no way to avoid being in violation of it from time to time? James is just trying to keep us from the silly rationalizations we use to make one sin seem more heinous than another. True, not all sins are the same as far as the ripple effect that they have on other people, but no sin is less guilt-deserving than another.

TEN COMMANDMENTS.
The well-known no-no's James mentions in verse 11—"Do not commit adultery" and "Do not murder"—are two of the Ten Commandments (Exodus 20:1-17).

Slavery or Freedom?

We've heard this term before: the "law of freedom" (1:25). But these two terms— "law" and "freedom"— don't sound like they belong together in the same sentence. Certainly to the unbeliever, or even to the Christian who's unwilling to deal with specific sins in his life, the commands of the Bible are nothing but unwanted limits and restrictions.

To the person wanting to gorge himself on alcohol, for example, God's warning against getting "drunk with wine" (Ephesians 5:18) stands in his way of having a good time. To the person wanting to get even with the girl who's been slandering her reputation, the Bible's command not to pay back "evil for evil or insult for insult" (1 Peter 3:9) doesn't give her much room to tell her what she really thinks.

But to Christians who truly desire to honor Christ, God's law is their protection, their ticket to contentment. It's the thing that helps them live with themselves when they go home at night. God's Spirit has transformed the way they look at what He expects. They know that the law is designed for *His* glory and *their* good.

FREEDOM IN CHRIST.
This was a big theme of the Apostle Paul's writings and ministry—that we were free from having to earn our way to salvation and free to serve God because of His Spirit's power within us. "For you are called to freedom, brothers; only don't use this freedom as an opportunity for the flesh, but serve one another through love" (Galatians 5:13).

Oh, Mercy

So, when you start to feel bad for being mean to somebody for no reason, or when you feel controlled by sinful desires that make you *so mad* when you give in to them, the Bible is your passport to freedom. It shows you how to confess your sins and restore a clear relationship with God. It inspires you to love and appreciate everyone no matter what they look like or how

MERCY.
The biblical concept of mercy means helping those who are in need or distress. In Jesus' life, of course, and in the forgiveness that flows from His death, we see mercy in its purest form—and we also see the basis for why we should show mercy to others.

much you are ridiculed for doing it.

But mercy must go both ways. Many believers today so abuse God's grace, they don't put up much of a fight against temptation, knowing God will be there to bail them out later. Yet these same people may be the ones who hold the longest grudges, who refuse to forgive others the way they themselves have been forgiven. To repent of our sins without allowing others the same privilege is a spiritual contradiction.

God's Word proves that "mercy" really is better than "judgment"—whether it's the joy you feel when you show mercy to others or the joy you feel in your own heart when God shows mercy to you.

TWO-WAY FORGIVENESS.
This thing about showing mercy and being forgiving of others is most clearly stated in the Lord's Prayer, where Jesus teaches us to pray to the Father, "Forgive us our debts, as we also have forgiven our debtors" (Matthew 6:12). Also check out the parable of the unforgiving slave (Matthew 18:21-35) and see how ugly our unforgiveness can look.

> Why is mercy stronger than judgment? Have you ever seen this truth portrayed in a movie or in a real-life event that you were a part of? What's it really like when mercy wins out?
>
> _____
> _____
> _____
> _____
> _____
> _____

2:14-19 Faith and Works

The Christian Connection
Some people think of Christians as people who are always *against* something: abortion, homosexuality, pornography, R-rated movies, and soccer games on

Sunday morning. It's true that part of our calling as believers is to stand up against cultural trends and ways of thinking that bring harm to the human race and mock the God we love and serve.

But this remaining section of James 2 is a clear challenge for us to be known by what we *do*, not by what we *don't* do. Our "faith," James says, should have a fair share of "works" to back it up.

Verse 14. Does this mean, then, that we can be saved by being good enough? I thought salvation was a gift from God—"not from works, so that no one can boast" (Ephesians 2:9). You're right. But this passage and the ones that follow are not talking about the initial faith in God that helped to save you. James is talking about the faith that continues to grow and increase in your life as you learn to trust Him and obey Him more fully. This is the faith that's still working ten, twenty, eighty-two years after you've come to Christ, always ongoing, always developing new muscles.

MARTIN LUTHER.
This outspoken Christian from the early 1500s was known for having trouble with the book of James, especially its statements that "faith without works is dead." His understanding of salvation by faith alone seemed incompatible with James's logic (although we'll see later how these two concepts go together). His work and writings were instrumental in the split between Catholics and Protestants, known in history as the Reformation.

Visible Need, Visible Faith

Perhaps you've been on a mission trip to an impoverished country or to a poor region of America—perhaps into the housing projects of your own hometown. You've seen the muddy faces, the often filthy living conditions, the hunger and extreme want. How did you feel about it? Did it make you want to help? Did it make you feel decadent to live in a place where you're always within minutes of a McDonalds?

What was your response to those feelings? Sure, you couldn't totally make things better for those in need.

CARE FOR THE POOR.
Being generous and openhearted toward the needy has always been a clear command from God and a hallmark of His people. See it spelled out way back in Deuteronomy 15:7-11.

You couldn't give the kids their father back if they didn't even know who he was. You didn't have enough money to buy them a nice new place to live. But you did do everything you could to help. You gave them something to eat, to drink. You smiled and hugged them. You made them feel loved.

So ask yourself this: would your faith in Christ be what it should be if you could find yourself in a situation like that—and *not* want to help—to just *act* like you care?

FAITH AT WORK.
For another twin-lens look at the marriage between faith and works, turn to 1 John 3:17-18 and see how serious the Scripture can be about putting these two together.

Faith Alone Doesn't Work

James had probably seen the same things we've seen: people who claim to have a belief in God but whose lives show nothing to support it. Why isn't this considered totally insane? Should we expect a girl who wants to be a nurse to hate the sight of blood? Should we expect a guy who says he loves baseball not to want to watch the World Series? Should we expect a kid who's crazy about computers not ever to be on it? Why, then, don't we expect Christian faith to lead logically to Christian actions?

We can understand why this might have been an issue at the time James wrote his letter. He was primarily writing to Jewish believers, many of whom were still struggling with the idea of Gentiles (non-Jews) being considered "brothers" in Christ. These Gentiles were more free by nature, more apt to be faith-based, less likely to want to win points with God by keeping the law. They tended to believe that faith outweighed works in importance, while others lived by the motto that actions speak louder than words.

The church still lives with this conflict. Even though we all pretty much agree on the big, important things, we each bring a little different spin to our Christian life. Based on the type of family we've come from or the culture we've been raised in, we may come down heavier on the side of works than faith or of faith than works.

But to James, "faith" and "works" were not separate menu options. A Christian couldn't have one without the other.

Wicked Faith

To drive this point monstrously home, James took his argument to the extreme. He asked the faith-only folks to meet some buddies of theirs who agreed with them—the "demons" in hell. Yes, Satan and his evil, perverted agents *also* have faith alone.

But even wicked spirits will tell you that belief by itself—belief only in the existence of God—only makes them shudder. Mere belief that never has any intention of a changed lifestyle produces nothing but misery. John Milton has accurately pegged Satan and his demons. In *Paradise Lost* Satan says, "Better to reign in hell than to serve in heaven." This is the root of sin. This is the attitude that each of us has as children of Adam. However, faith in Christ—belief in who He is and all He's done—produces works of righteousness in us. Experiencing what it's like to live for Him causes us to love Him. Our "faith" makes us want to "work."

GOOD PEOPLE.
Ask a lot of people if they think they're going to heaven, and they'll tell you they think so ... because they try to be good people. But although being good—"having works"—is an important part of Christian "faith," it's not enough on its own to earn salvation, because "there is no one righteous, not even one" (Romans 3:10). We are all in need of God's forgiveness. And only those who trust in Christ will escape His judgment (John 3:18).

DEMONS.
These agents of Satan—also known as fallen angels—are active, evil beings who work against God's people but are limited by the power and authority of Christ. Their time is short, however, for there is an "eternal fire prepared for the Devil and his angels" (Matthew 25:41) where they will spend forever in torment.

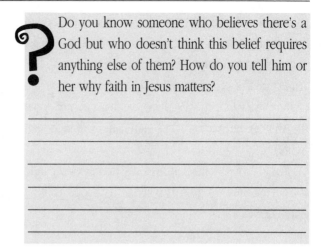

Do you know someone who believes there's a God but who doesn't think this belief requires anything else of them? How do you tell him or her why faith in Jesus matters?

2:20-26 Hall of Faith Moments

Abraham

If the "shudder" of the evil spirits is Exhibit A in James's argument that "faith" and "works" go hand in hand, Exhibit B comes from Genesis 22. This is where God told Abraham to take his only son, Isaac, to the top of a mountain and to sacrifice him there as a burnt offering. At first glance this sounds like a cruel trick on God's part, but we know from Hebrews 11:17-19 that He was in reality testing Abraham's faith.

James says that Abraham's willingness to obey at all costs "perfected" his faith (even though, as you know, God spared him at the last minute from actually killing Isaac). Abraham's action proved that his faith was real. It brought his belief full-circle. Had he not been able to trust God with his son's life, Abraham's faith would not have been complete.

So we learn from this story that faith and works are not either-or propositions. To have faith means that

ABRAHAM.
He was the first of the biblical patriarchs (PAY-tree-arks)—fathers of the faith who represented the early generations of God's people. Much as George Washington is considered the father of America, Abraham was that and more to the nation of Israel, for he was called by God into the role (Genesis 12:1-3), and his son Isaac was the first-born of the Jewish line.

faithful actions will follow.

No, good deeds alone don't count for anything.

Yes, faith is necessary before we can perform the kind of works that please God.

But when both come together—when faith inspires obedience—it's a living picture of true Christianity.

James vs. Paul

Now we come to a place where it's really easy to get confused.

James quotes an Old Testament passage (Genesis 15:6) as evidence "that a man is justified by works and not by faith alone." But this sounds almost exactly opposite to what Paul wrote. In fact, Paul used this same Genesis verse about Abraham to "conclude that a man is justified by faith apart from works of the law" (Romans 3:28).

So which one is it, guys? Are we justified by works? Or by faith?

The answer is all in the definitions . . .

Faith and Works, Justified

Faith. James is speaking of "faith" as mere intellectual belief in God's existence—a faith that can't save you. Paul uses "faith" to describe a person's belief in the saving work of Jesus Christ—His death and resurrection, His forgiveness of our sins.

Works. The "works" James talks about are the good deeds that should naturally flow out of a Christian's faith. Paul, however, is talking about a different kind of "works," warning his readers not to trust in the legalistic obeying of rules as a way of being saved from sin.

GOD'S FRIEND.
God specifically mentioned that Abraham was His "friend" (Isaiah 41:8), as was the Old Testament hero, Moses (Exodus 33:11). But Jesus declared to His disciples that they, too, were His "friends" (John 15:15), which includes all of us who trust in and follow Him.

PAUL'S DEFENSE.
Turn to Galatians 3:6-9 to see how Paul used this same verse about Abraham to argue that all those who have "faith"—not just the Jews—are received into God's family.

JUSTIFICATION.
This means being "declared righteous" by God (Romans 5:9), not as a result of our own efforts, but because of our faith in Christ. It doesn't mean we'll never sin again. But it does mean that at judgment God has promised to pronounce us innocent—our penalty bought and paid for by Christ's blood. Romans 5 is probably the best explanation of all this.

SANCTIFICATION.
This word is implied rather than expressed in James 2, but we'll go ahead and explain it anyway. This is the process of being made more and more holy—day by day—as we grow and mature as Christians. It begins at salvation and continues throughout our lives.

Justified. James is saying that we are "justified"—declared innocent by God—because our works prove that our faith in Him is genuine. Paul is also right, though, in saying that we are "justified" by what Christ has already done and by our faith in Him.

So Paul makes the case that we're not saved by our own good deeds. (Can't argue with that.) And James says that our good works will prove that our faith is real—to ourselves, to God, to everybody. (Shouldn't be able to argue with that either.)

Rahab

And finally, Exhibit C. The story of Rahab (found in Joshua 2) begins with the Israelites preparing to enter and conquer the Promised Land after forty years of wandering in the desert. Objective #1 was to take on the heavily fortified city of Jericho. Before sending the whole army out to war, however, Joshua dispatched a pair of spies to check out the city and see what God's people were up against.

But the foreign spies were spotted at the prostitute Rahab's house. It's not what you might be thinking, though. Rahab had called them in and hidden them on her rooftop from the local authorities, saving their lives in return for the safety of her family. She hoped the Israelites would spare her house when they descended on Jericho in battle. That's because, unlike others in her city, she believed that Israel's God was real, and she longed to be one of His people.

But if she had merely believed this without performing her brave act of heroism, her faith would have been seen as half-hearted. God tested her faith, and she responded with courageous obedience.

The Faith-Works Wrap-Up

Let's sum this section up. What do we call a body with no breath in it, with no movement, with no personality peeking through its face? Can a professing Christian who shows no sign of Christ's life inside be anything more than a spiritual corpse?

What do you think?

> Verses 14-26 give us a tough passage to understand. Has God cleared any of it up for you as you've studied it this closely? In what way?
>
> _____
> _____
> _____
> _____
> _____

LORDSHIP.
One of the conclusions you can draw from James's discussion about "faith" and "works" is that Jesus is more than our Savior; He is also our Lord (our King, our Ruler). Some people quibble over this, saying that it's wrong to add any other conditions to our salvation. But the Bible says that Jesus is "both Lord and Messiah" (Acts 2:36)—both our Master and our Redeemer. When we receive His salvation, we're also declaring that we intend to follow Him.

HALFTIME

This seems like a good spot—in light of James's statement that "faith without works is dead"—to think about what it really means to be alive in Christ.

More than likely, you know some people who don't have either faith or works—who are walking around looking full of life and fun and all, but who are dead and dying on the inside. They don't have Christ, and you know it.

You probably have other friends who may talk a good Christian game, but who sure don't live like it. As far as you can see, *faith* and *works* don't seem to match up in their average day. You get irritated with them sometimes. But deep down, you really want to help them see what life with Jesus can be like.

Or truth be told, maybe even you have been going to church and through all the right motions, but you've never really received God's forgiveness. Maybe you've been piling up some of the *works* part, but you've never attached *faith* to the equation.

So whether the Spirit is working on your own heart today, or whether He's bringing some other people's faces to mind as you think this over, let's take a quick swing back through the basics of salvation—to help us put it into words.

Here's the History

The Bible says that all around us—in the predictability of the sunrise, in the return of springtime, in the papery precision of a wasp's nest, in a thousand million ways—is the idea that God is living, active, and real, "being understood through what He has made." This is called *general revelation*—the fact that God's "eternal power and divine nature" have been made known to everyone. "As a result, people are without excuse" (Romans 1:20).

But in Jesus, God has made Himself fully known. "He is the image of the invisible God" (Colossians 1:15). "He is the radiance of His glory, the exact expression of His nature, and He sustains all things by His powerful word" (Hebrews 1:3). Every promise made to us by God has been fulfilled in Jesus Christ. This *special revelation* we have received by getting to see, hear, and know the Son of God brings us face-to-face with Him—as well as with ourselves.

Here's the Deal

(1) *In light of His perfection, then, we find ourselves to be sinners*—"guilty" even before we were born; already "sinful" when our mothers conceived us (Psalm 51:5). "There is no one righteous, not even one" (Romans 3:10). "All have sinned and fall short of the glory of God" (Romans 3:23).

(2) *In light of His coming to earth, though, we find ourselves loved*—for when the time was just right, "God sent His Son, born of a woman, born under the law, to redeem those under the law, so that we might receive adoption as sons" (Galatians 4:4-5). "We love because He first loved us" (1 John 4:19).

(3) *In light of such grace, we find ourselves needing to repent and believe*—" 'The message is near you, in your mouth and in your heart.' . . . If you confess with your mouth, 'Jesus is Lord,' and believe in your heart that God raised Him from the dead, you will be saved" (Romans 10:8-9).

(4) *So in light of His death—if we believe in Him—we will find ourselves forgiven*—"For rarely will someone die for a just person . . . but God proves His own love for us in that while we were still sinners Christ died for us" (Romans 5:7-8). "He has rescued us from the domain of darkness" and forgiven our sins (Colossians 1:13-14).

(5) *And in light of His resurrection—again, if we believe in Him—we can find ourselves unafraid*—for He has "abolished death and has brought life and immortality to light" (2 Timothy 1:10). "O Death, where is your victory? O Death, where is your sting?" We now have "victory through our Lord Jesus Christ" (1 Corinthians 15:55-57).

Jesus has done it all—lived a perfect life, died in our place, defeated death, and won for us an eternity with Him in heaven. The One who made us has come to save us . . . because He loves us.

What Do You Say?

If you're just now coming around to believing this for the first time, then pray this prayer right now. Or if you're sharing these truths from God's Word with someone else, show them how they can receive Christ just by saying something like this:

Lord God, You have shown me today that I have no hope without you. I can't keep from sinning and messing up. It's part of who I am. And so I give up trying to make myself a better person. Instead, I need You to make me a new person. I confess my sins. I believe in You—in Your life, in Your death, in Your return from the grave. And I am ready to receive the salvation You have promised—a life of peace and joy on earth, a life of unending love with You forever. Come into my heart, Lord Jesus. I need You—now!

James 3

3:1-2 Teaching Ambitions

Think before You Speak

Perhaps you've thought about becoming a teacher. Or even if you don't think you're going that way as a career, perhaps you'd like to work with students at church someday or teach a Sunday School class or lead a Bible study.

Well, don't just leap into that like it's no big deal, because there's a high level of responsibility that goes along with teaching. James says it puts you under a more high-powered microscope than it does for other people.

That's because teachers have an enormous influence over those who listen to them—for good or for bad. They no longer just speak for themselves; they also have a stake in how their words are received, understood, and acted upon.

Take, for example, a teacher who's a real truth-teller, who understands the Bible and practices Christ's principles in her behavior and attitudes. Compare her to another teacher who's into some kind of false religion, who has her own agenda, who denies the deity of Christ or thinks that all ways lead to God. How many people are affected by the things these teachers say and do? And how many others will their influence spread to through the students they've had in class?

So if you want to be a teacher, that's good. But take it seriously. God does.

TEACHING.
For the Jewish people living in New Testament times, most of the teaching was done at the local synagogue (SIN-uh-gog)—what we'd think of as a church building. Most of the instruction, then, was religious in nature. Teaching was also a primary function of pastors in the early church, although James's warning in verse 1 implies that volunteers could also apply for teaching duties.

Verse 1. What kind of "judgment" is James talking about here? Does this mean that on judgment day, God will require teachers to own up for all the things they've said? Surprise! All of us "will have to account for every careless word [we] speak" (Matthew 12:36). Although our souls will be saved if we are believers in Christ, God will still "test the quality" of what we've done on earth and reward us accordingly (see 1 Corinthians 3:12-15). So a teacher will indeed be judged on the final day for the things she taught and will also be held to a higher standard by both God and everyone else during this lifetime.

Say It Like You Mean It

Speaking of teachers (and watch out—pretty soon James's words will apply to all of us), James makes a very practical statement about their role and responsibilities. Because their mouths are the chief tools of their trade, they get the chance every day to practice one of life's most difficult self-disciplines: keeping their tongues under control.

In fact, if you really want a good test to see how completely submitted your will is to God's, measure it by your ability to keep from saying things you shouldn't. This is a true mark of Christian maturity.

How do you talk about your youth pastor? Your music leader? Your mom and dad? Your brothers and sisters? Your friends—even your *best* friends? Students at your school or people you don't even know? What do your answers tell you about the control you have over your mouth?

MATURITY.
One of the biggest problems in the church today is the lack of growth in many of its members —the expectation that just showing up on Sunday yet staying basically unchanged the rest of the week ought to pass as normal Christianity. Hebrews 5:11-14 talks about what God requires, not just of preachers and missionaries, but of everyone who claims Christ as Lord.

> Is controlling your tongue a real challenge for you? When do you sense it the most?

3:3-6 The Tongue Is Like . . .

Out of Control

There are so many things we can choose to do with the letters and syllables that come out of our mouths. And the Bible has a comment to make on just about all of them:

- *Lying.* "A lying tongue hates those it crushes" (Proverbs 26:28).
- *Gossip.* "A gossip separates friends" (Proverbs 16:28).
- *Slander.* "Whoever spreads slander is a fool" (Proverbs 10:18).
- *Cursing.* "There is one who speaks rashly, like a piercing sword" (Proverbs 12:18).
- *Wisdom.* "Knowledgeable lips are a rare treasure" (Proverbs 20:15).
- *Boldness.* "We speak, not to please men, but rather God" (1 Thessalonians 2:4).
- *Encouragement.* ". . . in order to give grace to those who hear" (Ephesians 4:29).
- *Honesty.* ". . . speaking the truth in love" (Ephesians 4:15).

THE SMALL STUFF.
The Bible is one story after another of how God made big things come from small packages. He tells us about the little kid brother who became the great King David (1 Samuel 16:1-13), the little town of Bethlehem that became the birthplace of Jesus (Micah 5:2), the little sack lunch Jesus used to feed more than 5,000 people (John 6:5-13). Get the idea?

From one end of the Bible to the other, God teaches us that this little tongue we carry around in our mouths tells a lot about what's going on in our "whole body." It is a prime indicator of the condition of our hearts. It may be small, but it is mighty powerful. "Avoid someone with a big mouth" (Proverbs 20:19).

Mini Lessons to Learn

Let's go inside these three quick examples of little things that pack a lot of power:

A horse's bit. You probably already know this, but a "bit" is a metal rod (attached to the bridle) that's placed inside a horse's mouth so that with one tug of the reins, the rider can make the horse change direction or stop. The bit is just a short, little hunk of steel. You can weigh it in ounces, not pounds. But it's powerful enough to make a 1,500-pound animal stop dead in its tracks.

A ship's rudder. This little blade that hangs underwater from the stern of a boat (the back, for you landlubbers) doesn't just stir the water at the rear. When the guy at the helm shifts the rudder, the head of the boat (and therefore, the whole boat itself) begins to turn in whatever direction he wants.

A forest spark. We've all seen how wildfires can spread across miles of timberland, threatening homes and wildlife, leveling everything in its path, roaring in laughter at man's best attempts to contain or extinguish it. And many times, the origin of such devastation is a single match strike, a hot cigarette ash, a lone, lingering spark from a campfire.

HORSES.
The horse was likely introduced into the Middle East around 2,000 years before Christ. It was primarily used for riding, for transporting goods, and for its strength and speed in warfare. King Solomon had as many as 12,000 horses that were used to pull chariots.

SHIPS.
By Roman times, the seas and rivers were busy places, with water travel and trade being conducted along the many ports and harbors throughout the Middle East. That's why just about everyone would have been familiar with James's analogy of the ship's rudder [verse 4].

The Tongue's Heat Source

In purely physical terms, the tongue is nothing more than a movable muscle that helps us slurp on a straw, lick envelopes, and form phonics sounds. It's a pretty cool thing God created, but it's not something you think about a lot, unless you happen to bite it real hard by accident. *(Ouch!)*

But James has a way of describing the tongue, which seems way out of proportion to its size. He calls it a "world of unrighteousness"—a brewing, smoldering mass of potential destruction—able to poison our hearts and change the course of our lives.

Some of us know this more than others. Some have been verbally abused by a parent, an older sibling, or a school bully. Some have been constantly demeaned and demoralized by an authority figure. But all of us in some way or another have felt the bitter taste of hateful speech, which is "set on fire by hell" itself.

HELL.
The Greek word for "hell" in verse 6 is gehenna—the "valley of Hinnom"—a ravine on Jerusalem's south side once used for pagan worship and (in James's day) converted to a garbage dump.

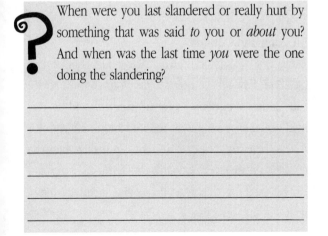

When were you last slandered or really hurt by something that was said *to* you or *about* you? And when was the last time *you* were the one doing the slandering?

3:7-12 More Takes on the Tongue

Whoa, Big Fella!

Never at a loss for an analogy, James moves beyond little things like horse bits and boat rudders, painting our tongues in a wide range of wild animal prints. Like leopards and tigers. Falcons and vultures. Snakes and lizards. Sharks and piranhas. Even in Bible times, apparently some of these kinds of critters had been harnessed and put to use by man. Certain animals had been tamed enough to work on man's behalf or fetch sticks for man's enjoyment.

"But no man can tame the tongue." Controlling our speech is the endless work of a lifetime. We can get better at it, but we never outgrow our need to keep an eye on it, to lock it up when we're not on guard, to beware lest it turns on us.

TAMING ANIMALS.
The animals most commonly tamed in Bible days for use in domestic tasks—or as household pets—were the donkey, camel, cow, dog, goat, horse, ox, sheep, and pig.

POISON.
This death-carrying concept was a common biblical description for the lethal power of a person's words [Psalm 140:3].

Blessing and Cursing

James is so good about giving us vivid teaching examples. He draws these quick, little word pictures so we can understand deep, spiritual concepts—ideas that might otherwise sail by us, ignored and unnoticed.

But here he presents us with a reality even he couldn't understand: how any one item—the tongue—can be used for such good things and such bad things, nearly at the same time.

IN GOD'S IMAGE.
What does it mean to be made "in God's likeness" [verse 9]? Among the best answers are things like: each of us is unique, able to think and analyze and remember things from the past, created with a purpose given to us before birth by God. Even those who reject their Maker cannot shake the fact that they owe their very life to Him [Romans 1:25].

Verse 10. This verse sets up a tension in all of us that must be addressed and (hopefully) corrected. Do you have a *campus* lifestyle and a *church* lifestyle? Are you the same person when you're out on Friday night as you are on Sunday morning? If you know you're two different people when you're in different places, then you need to deal with this statement: "Things should not be this way." There are few things in life more liberating than the freedom of being *who* we are *wherever* we are. And as Christ gains control of our tongues, the people at school should be able to see it just as well as the people at church.

In Your Choice of Flavors?

Remember in chapter 2 when James talked about "faith" and "works"? His argument then was that "works" ought to follow "faith" like three follows two, like summer follows spring, like Monday follows Sunday. It ought to be natural. Even a fool knows that.

Using the same kind of logic in teaching on the tongue, James points here and there, asking us to think for a second. Does saltwater come out of a mountain spring? Do olives grow on a fig tree? Do dates sprout from a grapevine?

Do you study *The Scarlet Letter* in chemistry class? Do you play football on a dance floor? Do you dress in formal wear for phys ed? Some things just don't go together, and everybody knows it!

Common sense tells us (if nothing else does) that our tongues were not designed to be schizophrenic. They were *created* by God to bring *glory* to God.

SPRINGS.
In the hot, dry, desert conditions of the Middle East, these underground fountains—that formed naturally in the limestone rock of that region—were highly prized as water sources. In the vivid language of the Bible, springs were also synonymous with God's care and blessing.

FIG TREES.
These stumpy, gnarly trees with thick branches and twigs produced a favorite fruit of biblical times, especially because the figs dried well and could be stored in cakes. (Kinda makes me want a fig newton!) Jesus referred to figs and fig trees several times (Luke 21:29).

NATURAL WORLD.
One of God's reasons in creating the physical world was to show us what He is like and how His truth operates, "being understood through what He has made" (Romans 1:20). Every time you recognize that a flower grows upward toward the sun, or how a tree is restored to life in the spring, or why a bird goes to such lengths to provide shelter and nourishment for her young, you're seeing God's nature and order in action. Be sure to keep an eye out for it.

 What are some things you've noticed in the natural world that teach you something about who God is, or what He's like, or how life is supposed to work?

_____
_____
_____
_____
_____
_____

3:13-15 Real Wisdom and Real Problems

Heavenly Wisdom

Do you know someone who is "wise and understanding"? How do you know this about them? Is it because they always seem to have the right answers? Is it because they know the Bible so well? Do they just seem so smart about so many things?

We tend to think of wisdom and understanding as being nothing more than knowledge, an ability to handle big thoughts and express them in big words. But wouldn't you expect James (from what you've seen of him so far) to cut through all the fancy talk and flowery language and to point out the "wise and understanding" people in terms we could all understand?

I'll tell you who's wise and understanding, he says—people who know what's right and do it. People who do what's right but don't go around telling you how right they are.

ALL-WISE.
Among the most powerful passages of worship in all the Bible is Romans 11:33-36—an outburst of praise, made right in the middle of Paul's writing. It reveals God as a boundless source of "wisdom" and "knowledge." Truly, He is the "only wise God" (Romans 16:27).

Wisdom and understanding, he says, are a lot less about big talk and a lot more about "good conduct."

Envy and Ambition

Now meet the two worst enemies of wisdom and understanding:

ENVY.
As a way of showing just how snide and sneaky this rotten character trait can get, the Apostle Paul said that some people even "preach Christ out of envy and strife" (Philippians 1:15). Apparently, no one is immune from being bitten by the "bitter envy" bug.

- *"Bitter envy"* is that squinty-eyed hatred for what others have (like big money, straight teeth, and a date on Friday night) or for what others can do (like play the piano, make people laugh, or outrun you in track).

- *"Selfish ambition"* is the me-first motivation that's always looking for an angle, a way to make ourselves look better or to get an advantage over someone else.

These are not outright sins, you might say, like lying, stealing, or cheating on math tests. No, they're sneakier than that. They even disguise themselves as good behavior, like when you offer to do something nice for your teacher in hopes of getting a better grade. Or when you invite someone over (which is really outgoing of you) but not because you really like or care about this person. You just want others to think you're best buds.

James is saying that the Christian life is not plastic and flimsy. Spiritual success can't be measured simply by whether or not people think we're good kids. If we do a lot of nice, acceptable things for all the wrong reasons, we're living "in defiance of the truth"—the truth that Christian character should go to the bone.

DEMONIC.
Satan and his demons are busy and active in this world, "working in the disobedient" (Ephesians 2:2), hoping to turn our hearts away from devotion to God and toward our own pet projects of hate, anger, jealousy, and discord. With Christ inside us, though, we have the power to "resist" them and all his tricks (4:7).

Evil Unintentions

You wouldn't think it, maybe, but when we do good things just to be noticed or to get what we want, our hearts are slithering into areas that are "earthly" (short-sighted), "sensual" (based on nothing but our feelings), and even "demonic" (playing right into Satan's hands).

When we do this, we're not just innocently doing what everybody else is doing. We're being led around by the Devil's lies and working hard against the plans God has for us.

> Have you caught yourself planning to do something for no other reason than what others would think? Or to get something for yourself out of it? Describe how rotten that feels.

3:16-18 Satan's Wisdom and God's Wisdom

No Middle Ground

James is describing two different kinds of "wisdom"—a pure wisdom that leads us to humbly obey God for His approval alone and a polluted non-"wisdom" that leads us to go after whatever we want, to put ourselves before our faith.

The trouble with this second "wisdom" is that we have no idea how far away from God it'll take us. "For where envy and selfish ambition exist," anything can happen.

"Disorder," for example, comes from a word that can be translated "confusion." It's the idea of trouble, disturbance, instability, anarchy. It's not as though Christians who start habitually giving in to their own feelings become experts in "every kind of evil." But they're definitely heading that direction. Who knows how far away from God they'll wander before the consequences catch up with them?

That's because there's no middle wisdom—no sorta-this and sorta-that. We're either growing in God's direction, opening ourselves up to new opportunities for ministry and joyful service, or bending away from God's blessings toward a bottomless pit of wasted potential.

SELFISH AMBITION.
This look-at-me mentality shows up in Paul's list of Christlike opposites, along with the big boys of sexual immorality, promiscuity, sorcery, drunkenness, and a bunch of other bad stuff (Galatians 5:19-21). Consider it part of the junk food to avoid while you're piling up the "fruit of the Spirit" on your clean plate of new character traits (Galatians 5:22-23).

Spiritual Character Award

When we truly seek God's brand of "wisdom," look what we become:
- *Pure*—sincere, moral, genuine, authentic.
- *Peace-loving*—promoting harmony in all our relationships.
- *Gentle*—considerate of others, not harsh or cutting down.
- *Compliant*—approachable, obedient, willing to learn.
- *Full of mercy and good fruits*—faithful, focused, and forgiving.
- *Without favoritism and hypocrisy*—single-minded, consistent, kind to everybody.

Normal human living is unspiritual, self-centered, and oriented toward personal gain. It's concerned only with physical needs and urges. It's driven by immediate wants and wishes. But God offers us something so much better—a life that's bigger than the next forty-eight hours. Relationships that go deep and stay strong. A character that looks as good on you now as it will for a lifetime. And even for an after-lifetime.

Best of all, it's not a huge effort. It's just the natural "fruit of righteousness" that grows in the hearts of those who love God, who sow their time and energies into serving Him.

> Look at the six-piece set of virtues from the previous section. Which of these character traits do you most desire from God? How would these change your life for the better?

James 4

4:1-5 Why We Fight

The Source of Conflict

Having a hard time getting along with somebody? Are you starting to hate people who take a particular stance on a certain issue? Are you snubbing other believers who are struggling right now, who aren't doing what you think they should do?

If you're answering "yes" to questions like these—and you want to know why—James says to start by looking inside yourself, at the "war within you." Is part of the reason you're in conflict with others because you want to control them? Is it because they're not giving you what you want? Is it because they're costing you more time, energy, and patience than you want to pay?

Remember, James just got through talking in 3:18 about "those who make peace"—those who are so at peace with God and with themselves, peace simply flows out through their words and behavior. Peace is their first reaction. This doesn't mean we can never confront. It doesn't mean that whatever anybody wants to do ought to be OK with us.

But it does mean that our first concern should always be for others, not for ourselves—for God's will to be done, not ours.

THE WAR WITHIN.
You've certainly noticed—like all of us do—how hard it is to live what we believe because of the battle we fight inside ourselves. Paul does a good job of explaining this war between our two natures—our Spirit nature and our human nature—in Romans 7:14-25.

COVETING.
This is the last [but not least] of the Ten Commandments, found in Exodus 20:17. It's not just the idea of liking the car somebody drives, but of wanting one so badly that you'll go into debt, get into trouble, or pout and make everyone miserable till you get one.

MURDER.
You probably remember how Jesus equated murder with unsettled anger in Matthew 5:21-22. We may not be as innocent of this high-profile crime as we think we are.

The Character of a Craving

This battle you may be fighting inside can take several forms:

• *"You desire and do not have."* This is another way of describing the "bitter envy" James talked about in 3:14. There are things you want, but you can't get your hands on them, and this makes you feel less than friendly toward those who have what you crave.

• *"You murder and covet and cannot obtain."* I doubt you've been going around killing people, but James's graphic language was no accident. The jealous attitude that makes us want things we don't have is the same one that drives people to drastic measures, like stealing and murdering. If you've ever wanted something so badly—like popularity or the ability to make people laugh—that you've started despising those who have it, then you know the feeling. If you'd do anything you could to bring that person down, you've let your love for some thing turn into hatred for the person who has it.

• *"You do not have because you do not ask."* The main reason we "fight and war" with others is because we want the wrong things. Since we want the wrong things, we have to go somewhere besides God to get them. This happens when our hearts aren't asking for things that would bring glory to God but glory to ourselves—like when a girl feels attracted to a guy who doesn't love Christ, but she wishes he would ask her out anyway.

God, you remember, "gives to all generously" (1:5). Everything we really need, God freely gives to us. We don't have to go out begging for it, arguing about it, or chewing people up over it. If it has to be gotten that way, it's not worth having.

What does God give us? "Wisdom from above" (3:17)—the wisdom to live for Him in a personal relationship where we look to Him for everything.

When Prayer Goes Bad
Sometimes, though, just going to God is not enough. Sometimes our praying is little more than a scheme to get God to work for us. But guess what? God is not a snack machine who coughs up candy bars just because we put three quarters in.

If there are things you want from God just so you can "spend it on your desires for pleasure," you can expect to be turned down flat. If you want $35 just because you're embarrassed to tell your friends you can't afford to go somewhere, then you've got an internal war on your hands. If you pray your parents will give you permission to do something you probably shouldn't do, you're probably not going to get it. Either way, you're likely going to be raising your voice and causing a stink while you're trying.

Verse 3. If I don't get something I ask God for, does that mean I must be "asking wrongly"? Let's say I've been praying for a friend of mine to become a Christian, but she hasn't. How could my motives be wrong in that? Well, just because a prayer isn't answered the way we think it should be, that's not an automatic slap against our selfishness. Sometimes He knows that what we really need most is just a little more patience.

ANSWERED PRAYER.
It may seem like God isn't listening. Sometimes His silence is hard to understand. But the Bible promises in numerous places (like Psalm 34:17) that "the Lord hears" us when we pray. So believe it, even when you can't feel it.

SELFISH WANTS.
To see the raw results that come from wanting things our way—no matter what others think or say—flip back to Luke 15:11-24 and read Jesus' story of the runaway son.

COVENANT RELATIONSHIP.
This idea of being unfaithful to God—as though we were His bride—is rich in Old Testament thought (like in Isaiah 54:5-8) and descriptive of His great love for us. For an incredible, real-life story about this, spend some time in Hosea 1–3. You won't believe it!

ASCETICISM.
Many people throughout history—and even some today—have felt that the only way to avoid being "the world's friend" is to totally remove themselves from society or go to severe lengths to deprive themselves of comfort, food, or shelter. This is commonly known as asceticism (uh-SET-ih-SIZ-um). Though it's probably not misguided in all cases, it does seem to contradict Jesus' prayer for His disciples in John 17:15.

Friends of Men, Friends of God

"Adulteresses!" Wow. Talk about your shock value! But that's the label James hangs on people who play around with sin and selfishness while they're supposed to be staying faithful to the one true God. It's like having an affair—or, let's call it what it really is: cheating on Jesus.

Our culture likes to make a lot of exceptions, excuse a lot of gray areas, and exempt a lot of Christians from taking their faith too far. But James lays it out there without polish or apology—if we want to be the world's friend, then we'd better prepare to live with the fall-out: We've then become "God's enemy." Straight up. Black and white.

That's why James's appeal for us to seek God's wisdom is so serious. Every sin is forgivable, but that doesn't keep every sin from being a slap in God's face.

The Jealousy of God

How hot would the jealousy boil up inside you if you found out your boyfriend or girlfriend was seeing somebody else on the side? After all you've done, after all you've been to this person, how could he? How could she? How could someone do this to you!

Imagine, then, what goes through God's mind when we sin against Him—after all He's done for us, after all He's been to us.

There are several ways to look at verse 5, each of which is a shade different from the other. But basically, you get the picture. The Holy Spirit "yearns jealously" to win our hearts and affections, to make our love burn for Him and Him alone. He knows that He alone can satisfy us. He wants us spared from the nasty side-effects of selfishness. And He understands that our obedience is the only way for us to experience a relationship with Him.

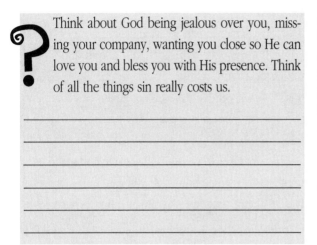

Think about God being jealous over you, missing your company, wanting you close so He can love you and bless you with His presence. Think of all the things sin really costs us.

4:6-10 Life in God's House

Greater Grace

The Bible is full of warnings and commands. The book of James is not the only place where the standards are high and the cost of disobedience severe.

Yet pinned on the top of everything God does is this incredible truth, which doesn't contradict His holiness but only heightens His power: "He gives greater grace." He understands that we're easily knocked off balance. He knows that surrender comes hard. "He knows what we are made of" (Psalm 103:14).

Those who insist on remaining "proud" and self-sufficient will find themselves facing the inevitable resist-

JEALOUS GOD.
It's weird to think of God being "jealous" (verse 5), but this is one of the ways He reveals Himself to us in the Bible—angry that His people have been lured away to worship idols and dabble in sin. Deuteronomy 4:23-24 is one of the many passages that explore this.

HOLY SPIRIT.
There is some dispute in the Christian community over when and to what degree the Holy Spirit comes "to live in us" (verse 5). Some believe—especially from several stories found in the book of Acts—that we receive the Spirit in His fullness at some point after salvation. Others believe that He enters our hearts at the moment of conversion as the "down payment" of our future reward (Ephesians 1:13-14). This would make a good study for you.

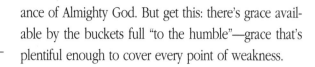

GRACE.
This is the undeserved acceptance and love of God—given to us through Christ's sacrifice for our sins—as well as His ongoing forgiveness and approval that motivates and inspires us to obedience [Titus 2:11-14].

HUMBLE.
Some people think humility means having a mousey, aw-shucks, low-level view of ourselves. Actually, it means understanding who we are in Christ—highly valued by our Creator and Savior, yet entirely dependent on Him and willing to put others first.

GREATER GRACE.
God's grace has the incredible quality of being able to stretch and grow beyond all limits, big enough to cover any sin, no matter how careless or cruel. "Where sin multiplied, grace multiplied even more" [Romans 5:20].

ance of Almighty God. But get this: there's grace available by the buckets full "to the humble"—grace that's plentiful enough to cover every point of weakness.

Go Do It

A little grammar lesson won't hurt you here. What do you call a sentence that starts with a verb and has an understood "you" as the subject—as in, "Take out the trash"? Got it yet? It's called a command or an imperative. It's one person telling another person to do something.

The sentences in verses 7-10 are one command after another—not to see how high you can jump but to see how you can grow as a Christian, how to push Satan and his sin-seducers into the trashcan they came from, how to experience the humility that welcomes God's everyday doses of grace.

Ten Steps to the Heart of God, Part 1

Count them up:

- *"Submit to God."* The word James used for "submit" comes from a military term that means to be "arranged or ordered under." It's all about aligning ourselves under another's authority. This really is step one in spiritual growth. The Christian life is not so much about committing ourselves as it is about submitting ourselves.

- *"Resist the Devil."* Some people think they're big and bold enough to take on the Devil in an all-out, storming-the-gates-of-hell rampage. In the name and strength of the resurrected Lord, we do possess that kind of ammo. However, James is sure right when he says that the best offense is a good defense, the God-powered privilege of seeing Satan coming—and telling him flat-out, "NO WAY!" just before he flees from us.

- *"Draw near to God."* We can't get close to God without our hearts being changed, without submitting our will to His and wanting to obey His Word. But we also can't draw near to God without God doing something He promises in return: to "draw near" to us.

- *"Cleanse your hands."* The most powerful tools we have for either sinning or serving are our own two hands. God commands us to do the hard work of keeping our lives clean and ready for Him to use.

- *"Purify your hearts."* But all the outward obedience in the world doesn't mean a lot unless our hearts are pure, unless our lives are free from "bitter envy" and "selfish ambition." A double-minded person, you'll remember, "is unstable in all his ways" (1:8).

DEVIL.
Known to us as Satan (meaning "adversary" or "enemy"), the Devil is a created being who rebelled against God's authority and led other fallen angels in revolt. He continues to oppose God's purposes in the world, though he is already defeated and merely biding his time.

CLEANSING.
We talked about this back in chapter 1, but you can tell how well James knows his audience by the way he talks about the importance of being cleansed and purified. The ancient, ceremonial laws of Israel were full of intricate details about what kinds of animals were clean and unclean, how to prepare oneself for worship, and many other things. Even the sanctuary itself had to be purified periodically from coming into contact with sinful man (Leviticus 16:15-19).

HOLY, NOT HAPPY.
Many people have a problem with God because they expect Him to always make them happy, to keep them at a certain level of comfort. Sure, God enjoys giving "good things" to His children, like any father would [Matthew 7:11]. But He's not averse to leading us through times of "mourning" [verse 9] or disciplining us for our own good [Hebrews 12:9-11]. He wants us holy—even when it hurts—because that's the only way to real happiness.

THE WAY UP.
For a very similar statement to verse 10—"Humble yourselves before the Lord, and He will exalt you"—look at Jesus' instructions on party manners [Luke 14:7-14] as well as His parable about the two praying men [Luke 18:9-14].

Ten Steps to the Heart of God, Part 2

The first five were all the ones you'd expect. But these sure aren't!

- *"Be miserable."* Hmm. Bet you never saw this one coming! It doesn't really mean that we're to make ourselves deliberately unhappy. That would go against other clear teachings of Scripture. This is probably talking about being willing to undergo hardship and persecution for Jesus' sake, rather than always defaulting to our own comfort and happiness.

- *"Mourn."* Again, this sounds absolutely ridiculous at first blush. But Jesus taught us, "Blessed are those who mourn, because they will be comforted" (Matthew 5:4). In other words, it's a sign of strength when your heart breaks over your own sin and over the havoc sin wreaks in the lives of your friends, your family, and the world in general.

- *"Weep."* Tears shouldn't be a total stranger in the eyes of a Christian. There are so many people hurting, so many people in need, so many times when we fail to follow our Lord like we should. Not everything in the world is good, and the pain that flows from this startling reality should be enough not only to get our attention but also our compassion.

- *"Your laughter must change to mourning."* To people who don't want to grow in the Lord, this stuff just sounds depressing. But there is maturity in learning that life is not a big joke and not everything is meant to be funny. Growing Christians can still be silly, but they also know how to be serious.

- *"Humble yourselves before the Lord."* Are we willing to trust God to meet our own needs His way? Or will we insist on thinking we know how to take care of ourselves a little better than He does? In choosing which question applies, remember this: if you'll willingly lay down your life for Him, "He will exalt you." And that's a promise.

> In thinking through James's recipe for healthy, mature Christian living, which ones have you actually tried to embrace? And what did God do in your life when you did?

_____

_____

_____

_____

_____

4:11-12 The Law and the Lawgiver

Back Off

Few things in life come quite so naturally to us as the desire to gossip and talk about other people. James, though—as you might imagine—was not the kind of guy who would give us the pass just because we have a built-in tendency to talk ugly. He has one basic word to say about it: "Don't."

Slander and criticism, James tells us, are not just attacks on others but also on God. When we come out in judgment of someone else, we're acting like we know as much as God does, like we can see into someone's heart and read their thoughts and motives.

THE LAW.
Think of this, not in terms of all the ceremonial laws from the Old Testament—many of which were fulfilled in Christ and are no longer in force (Colossians 2:16-17)—but as the revelation of God's will as it's told to us in the Bible, all the teachings and truths about Him.

But only God, who has given us "the law" of His Word to follow and obey, is able to judge a person where it counts, on the inside.

We've got all we can do just to obey the Scriptures ourselves, becoming "a doer of the law." Let's not take on the extra work of feeling responsible for deciding how well everybody else is doing it.

Verse 11. What room does this verse leave, then, for things like accountability groups? What am I supposed to do when another believer is doing something that's obviously against the Bible's teaching? Do I just stand there and act like nothing's wrong? No, God gives us the authority and wisdom to make value claims about certain behaviors, to "recognize" sinful desire by the "fruit" it produces in people's lives (Matthew 7:15-20). But we don't have the right (as God does) to determine whether a person will ultimately go to heaven or not. Yes, we should hold the Word in high esteem, and we should hold each other—and ourselves—accountable to it. But "mercy triumphs over judgment" (2:13), and mature believers do a lot more encouraging than they do confronting.

God's Business

Not just gossip but all our sins are the direct result of putting too little value on God and on others. Once we realize that God alone is Judge, we won't feel so free to take His place. And once we realize that each person is created in His image and has been given direct worth from God Himself, we won't be so quick to cut him down.

"Who are you to judge your neighbor" when God Himself has already taken the job?

Have you ever thought about the fact that when you're critical of someone else, you're doing something only God has the right to do? The Greek word for *judge* has a wide range of meanings. It can mean *analyze* or *evaluate*. Believers are called to do this (1 Corinthians 5:5 and 1 John 4:1). The word *judge* also means to *condemn* or to *avenge*. We are to leave these actions to God. Criticism should be constructive. When we give it, we need to be sure of the facts and we need to check our motives and the spirit in which the criticism is given. How does that change things for you?

SAVE AND DESTROY.
Fearing God may not seem like the kind of relationship we want with a Father who loves us. Yet, we need to let our respect and awe of God balance out our tendency to want Him to be cozy, soft, and grandfatherly. Rather than fearing the Devil, the Bible says we should "fear" the One who (as Matthew said, like James) "is able to destroy both soul and body" (Matthew 10:28).

4:13-17 The Illusion of Control

Where're We Going?

"Next year I'm getting a job so I don't have to beg my parents for money."

"Next spring, we're going to the beach for vacation. You want to come with us?"

"Next weekend my friends and I are having a party over at my house."

Remember James's theme from the last section—about not trying to do God's job for Him? Well, here he goes again, telling us not to assume that we can lay claim to tomorrow, or this afternoon, or thirty minutes from right now.

BUSINESS.
Most of the work done by people who lived in the first-century villages of the Middle East was farming, agriculture. But they did make items to sell, like pottery, cloth, as well as metal and wooden implements. Especially in the cities, trade and travel was more extensive, making James's story from verse 13 a slice-of-life experience for many of his readers.

Verse 13. Does this mean we're not supposed to make any plans? Ever? Should we never think ahead about what we're going to do in the future? Actually, the Bible talks a lot about being good managers of our time and resources, about being alert and watchful. So God is not against making plans. What this verse is trying to expose is the self-centered attitude of planning stuff without even considering what God would have us to do. James is trying to remind us that we're only here by God's love and permission, and we're not entitled to one breath or one footstep or one heartbeat without His say-so and provision.

Vanishing Smoke

Do you know what your great-great-grandfather looked like, or what he did, or where he lived? More than likely, you don't even know his name. So do you ever find yourself mourning for his death—this man who was your grandfather's grandfather? Of course not. There was a day, though—not as long ago as you'd think—when he never thought he'd be so quickly forgotten.

All of us are like that—like the fog you might see when you wake up early in the morning or late at night when you're coming home from a ballgame or an evening away. Give it half a day, though, and the sun's heat will melt the mist into nothing, not even leaving a trace of moisture to remember it by. In the big scheme of things, we're all "a bit of smoke," just like the billions of others who have lived on this earth (verse 14).

But we are not just "a bit of smoke" to God. We have the hope of eternity to look forward to. We'll get to live forever with our Savior in heaven. Yes, our life here is just a wink and a whisper, a puff of smoke, and we can never let ourselves forget that. But because of what Christ has done for us, we who believe in Him are eternal. Even great-great-grandfathers.

Not So Fast

"Instead, you should say, 'If the Lord wills, we will do this or that.'"

It doesn't have to be these very words—"if the Lord wills"—as though the words themselves have some sort of magic spirituality to them. But we do need to have this kind of heart—a continual attitude of submission to God's plan and His purposes.

MIST.
This idea of mist, fog, or vapor—a "bit of smoke" (verse 14)—is a fairly common biblical concept to describe things that are gone before you know it. Isaiah says our sins are like that when God forgives them (Isaiah 44:22), as are the prospects of those who insist on rebelling against the Lord (Hosea 13:3).

BOASTING.
Dizzy Dean, the legendary baseball pitcher, said, "It ain't bragging if you can do it." The bragging and boasting James has in mind is making claims about what we're going to do tomorrow. None of us can guarantee we will even be alive tomorrow. Our lives and all our abilities are in God's hands. If we boast, we should boast in Him [Psalm 44:8; Jeremiah 9:23-24].

Otherwise, we can count ourselves among the boastful and arrogant. Or, as James has the guts to say, we can consider ourselves "evil." That's because the state of mind that causes us to be proud and presumptuous is no different than the one that makes people commit the worst of sins.

"I'm praying that next year God will give me the chance to go on a mission trip with our church group. But it's all up to Him. I just want whatever He knows is best."

Yeah, that sounds more like it.

Peer Pressure
Doing only what "the Lord wills" is the kind of attitude a Christian simply must have. So when others start wanting you to do things on a whim, when they tempt you to do things you shouldn't, when they're always wanting to tie you down to the plans they've made for you, cling to verse 17.

When you know what you're supposed to do, when you know God's will is different from your friends' wishes, when you know what it means "to do good" in a particular situation—and you don't do it—"it is a sin." So when someone who's a strong believer—who never imagined himself having a desire for drugs or (of all things) ever becoming addicted to them—starts hanging around with someone who does, well … the next thing you know, he's likely to start thinking it won't hurt him. He'll convince himself he can handle it. Soon he'll watch the wheels fall off his morals, addicted not only to peer pressure but to something much worse than he imagined.

What God wants comes first. And the more you follow Him, the more His desires will become your own.

> **How can it be a sin *not* to do something?**
>
> _____
> _____
> _____
> _____
> _____
> _____

SINS OF OMISSION.
We're all familiar with the sins we're capable of committing: lying, arguing, backbiting, complaining. But there are also sins, like the ones James covers in verse 17, that are sinful because we don't do them—as in not being thankful, never showing up on time, not caring about others, rarely doing our work well. These are sins we "omit"—often called sins of omission—and they're just as deadly, just as bad, just as much in need of correcting as the others.

James 5

5:1-6 Taking It to the Rich

Making Good Money?

For most of us, the thought of having a lot of money wouldn't make us "weep and wail" but dance and sing. We wouldn't think too long and hard about the "miseries" of being rich but about the possibilities. Oh, the possibilities!

So why was James so down on wealth?

It's not the first time he's brought this up. Earlier, he told the rich (in 1:10-11) that they'd better not feel too special just because they have money. A little later (in 2:3-6) he cautioned the rich not to play favorites over the poor.

But he saved his most vivid warnings for these six verses, where he told them to be *very careful* about the corrosive grip money can have on the human heart and about the divisive results it can have on human relationships.

For Love of Money

Do you know people who are always borrowing from you but never paying you back? Do you have a friend who's always getting himself into debt . . . just to buy more junk he doesn't need?

We're living in a culture that's in love with money and with the things money can buy. But all our "silver and gold"—just like the "clothes" and all the other stuff

MOTH-EATEN.
James made several statements in his letter that are very similar to teachings of Jesus from the Sermon on the Mount (Matthew 5—7). This bit about "moth-eaten" treasures bears a remarkable resemblance to Christ's words from Matthew 6:19-21.

EMMAUS.
Wealth. This word picture about "wealth" being "ruined" [verse 2] may not make a lot of sense to us, since we don't think of gold and silver coins as being able to rot or wear out. But when you consider that much of the wealth of James's day was in land and crops, you can more easily see how wealth could easily be "ruined" by bad weather or insects that cause a poor year for farming.

we love so much—are just a hop and a jump from the garbage heap, where every last stitch and stack of it will be "moth-eaten" and "corroded."

It really doesn't matter how shiny and new and name-branded something may appear for the moment. Everything we own is in some stage of decay. And the sooner we realize how short-term our stuff is, the sooner we'll be able to start making investments in other people, giving and caring and being free from the "love of money"—which is "a root of all kinds of evil" (1 Timothy 6:10).

Verse 3. Is it wrong to be rich? If wealth is like "a witness against you" that can "eat your flesh like fire," does this mean a rich person is sure of being sent to hell? Nowhere in the Bible are the rich condemned just for having money. But they are warned that it's "easier for a camel to go through the eye of a needle than for a rich person to enter the kingdom of God" (Luke 18:25). And they are told to "be on guard against all greed" (Luke 12:15), not to "store up treasure" when God wants it used and given and invested and multiplied. Yes, there are rich people who are Christians, and there are poor people who are not Christians. But believers must never love their silver more than their Savior.

SILVER AND GOLD.
The money most often mentioned in the New Testament is the denarius (duh-NAIR-ee-us) —a silver coin usually minted in Rome and amounting to a day's wage for a common laborer. Gold was sometimes used as currency, too, but was also valuable (because it was so easily melted and shaped) when made into jewelry or other decorative implements.

LORD OF HOSTS.
The Bible attempts to describe God by the Hebrew word Sabaoth (suh-BAY-oth)— which in various passages can mean His rule over Israel's armies, His supremacy over the so-called gods of other nations, His role as the captain of the heavenly beings, and more. Let's leave it at this: the Lord of Hosts is Lord over everything!

Ripping People Off

Loving and craving money is bad enough, but one of the things that makes it even worse is when we want it bad enough to cheat and connive to get more.

God loves people. How many times in the book of James have we seen Him coming to the defense of the poor and helpless, the accused and insulted, the beat-down and the used-up? That's why you can see Him in verse 4 paying close attention to the "cries" of the "workers," to the "outcry of the harvesters"—people who've been taken advantage of.

Have you ever felt that way—like when somebody wants you around just because of something you have or something you can do for them? Or have you ever done it to somebody else—like when you've given a half-hearted effort but still expected full appreciation and payment?

Money has a way of bringing out the worst in us. So when our greed hurts another person, you can count on this: It reaches "the ears" of God.

Not a Pretty Picture

The goal of getting rich may have a nice gleam and sparkle about it to us. But from God's viewpoint, it looks a whole lot different. Instead of fun and games, He sees excessive luxury and indulgence. Instead of pleasure and satisfaction, He sees people getting fat and lazy, gorging themselves on their own selfish appetites.

Instead of winning the envy of our friends and neighbors, He sees foolish kids looking as stupid as sheep, blindly marching toward the "day of slaughter." Instead of earning points from all the right people, He sees the rich running rough-shod over "the righteous," thinking they're so superior when in fact they're sadly mistaken.

This money thing is just not as great as the Devil cracks it up to be. The only riches worth having are the "riches of [God's] grace," which He has "lavished on us with all *wisdom and understanding*" (Ephesians 1:8). Remember these very words from James 3:13-17. Wisdom and understanding are more important than all the money in the world.

GROWING FAT.

This is not the first time God's people have been described as growing fat and lazy. In Deuteronomy 32:15, Moses recounted how God had blessed them and blessed them and blessed them some more. Yet instead of being grateful and using His gifts, Israel had swallowed them whole and kept them all to themselves.

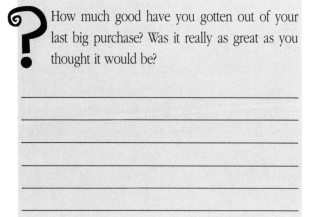

How much good have you gotten out of your last big purchase? Was it really as great as you thought it would be?

5:7-12 Hang In There

Willing to Wait

Instead of us wanting it all—and wanting it now—James gives us three pieces of good advice:

First, "be patient." Instead of demanding things from God—and feeling mistreated if He doesn't deliver—we should get used to the fact that God not only knows exactly what we need but also when we need it.

Are you sick and tired of wearing braces on your teeth? "Be patient." Are you not sure how much more bench-warming you can stand before you quit baseball? "Be patient." Are you longing for a day without curfews? "Be patient."

This cool Christian character trait of patience makes a handsome set when paired with humility—the unassuming trust factor that's been an underlying theme in the book of James. These twin strengths help believers move in the direction of being totally submitted to God's will. So try them on. They'll look really good on you.

The Big Payoff

But what reason do we have for being patient? How long do we need to wait before we can feel better about whining and worrying? That's where the second part of James's advice comes in: *"Be patient until the Lord's coming."*

Christians—more than anyone else—are able to live with an eternal perspective. If something doesn't work out in two weeks, that's OK. "The Lord's coming is near." If we don't get a quick "yes" answer to our

EARLY, LATE RAINS.
In New Testament Palestine, rain came primarily during two distinct seasons. The early rains arrived in October and November, and the late rains fell during February and March. Rarely was there any significant rainfall outside of these times of the year, so the local farmers planned around and counted on these rainy seasons in deciding when to plow.

prayer, we can live with that. "The Lord's coming is near."

This is not a cop-out. It's not an excuse to be lazy and not care, to settle for bad grades and sloppy performance. Instead, James calls it a reason to "strengthen [our] hearts," to live in obedience and hold on to God's encouragement. If our life doesn't track just the way we expected it would, we still have forever to love, serve, and worship the Lord. What's the hurry?

Verses 8-9. We know the book of James was written nearly 2,000 years ago. Was it just wishful thinking, then, when he said—in double digits A.D.—"the Lord's coming is near"? Were his signals crossed when, far in the distant past, he said, "The judge stands at the door"? Truth is, you've got to remember that our concept of time is different from God's. "With the Lord one day is like 1,000 years" (2 Peter 3:8). Eternity is so vast, so impossible to measure or to get our arms around, it's well inside the range of truth for Christ's coming to be "near" 2,000 years ago and still "near" this afternoon.

Quit Your Griping

In case we're not too keen on being patient, James's third word of advice stops us cold—before we can cave to one of our first natural reactions. Instead of taking our frustrations out on everybody else, he tells us not to *"complain about one another."*

Usually, when things are not going your way, you'll find somebody to blame: your parents, your siblings,

SECOND COMING.
Some think it's nonsense that Jesus is ever coming back to avenge sin. This position is exposed in 2 Peter 3:1-13, using Noah's generation as an example of those who scoffed at his warning yet paid a deep-water price. God's delay, though, is actually a sign of His mercy and patience, not His weakness. He will "come like a thief" and redeem His people.

HEAVENLY MINDED.
One of the common knocks against Christians is that we're "too heavenly minded to be of any earthly good." Some people accuse us of having our heads in the clouds, not having both feet in this world because we're putting all our stock in another one. It's true that we need to understand we have business to attend to while we're here. But what's wrong with looking forward to an eternity with Christ? Who's got a better plan for living than that?

GOD THE JUDGE.
Another routine question you're likely to field from Christianity critics is the one about how a loving God could send anyone to hell. A good response is to remind people that we're not as innocent as we think. Every one of us was born sinful (Psalm 51:5), deserving nothing but death (Romans 6:23). So the better question to ask is why God saves any of us at all! Those who go to hell have actually chosen it for themselves by rejecting Christ's forgiveness.

the guy you can't stand at school, the girl who's going with the guy you wish you were dating.

Even church can give you fuel for your venom:
- "I don't like the youth pastor."
- "This youth ministry isn't run right."
- "I don't like the worship."
- "All the students who come here are fakes."
- "The music in this place is just silly."
- "The retreats and stuff are too expensive."
- "I'm really frustrated with our pastor."
- "The people who help around here are mean."
- "I don't think there's enough Bible teaching."

But a day is coming—sooner than we realize—when everything is going to be sorted out, and the One who knows the hearts and minds of every person will make all things right. As Jesus said, "There is nothing covered that won't be uncovered, and nothing hidden that won't be made known" (Matthew 10:26). It's not up to us to be the reporter. Besides, how would you like it if people had a grouchy list about you?

Remember the question James asked in 4:12—"Who are you to judge your neighbor?" This also goes for the people who are making life really hard for you right now.

Enduring Examples

James put skin and bones on his three pieces of advice, backing them up with these testimonies of how they look and work in a person's life.

- *"The farmer."* Just about all of James's readers understood farm life, so they were well aware of what it was like to put seed in the ground and wait . . . wait

... wait all through the spring and summer until patience could bear its fruit and offer up its delicious reward. The final product never tastes as good, though, to the ones who grumble and grouch as it does to those who just keep on working and never quit trusting.

- *"The prophets."* The Old Testament prophets had the unenviable job of telling people the truth . . . whether the people wanted to hear the truth or not. So naturally, they had a way of ruffling feathers and rankling the tempers of men and women blinded by sin and unwilling to change. The prophets had to put up with a ton of ridicule and slander, but in the end they received the blessing of God's enduring reward. So it not only balanced out. It tipped in their favor.

- *"Job."* You may or may not know his story from the Old Testament book that bears his name. But Job (pronounced with a long "o," rhymes with "robe") was a godly man who had lots of bad things happen to him. Although he struggled mightily at times with the fallout of his great losses, God gave him the ability to see things from an eternal perspective and wait patiently on his Lord.

Sum it all up, and it looks like this: Life may seem tough and very hard to take right now. But no matter how things may appear, you can be sure that you serve a God who is "compassionate and merciful," who hasn't forgotten what you're going through but is growing something valuable inside of you . . . if you'll ask him for the strength to be patient (Proverbs 19:11; Romans 5:3-5; Hebrews 10:36).

SUFFERING PROPHETS.
One of the prophets who endured repeated persecution at the hands of the people was Jeremiah, who was threatened with death (Jeremiah 26:7-15), thrown into jail (Jeremiah 37:11-16), and tossed into an empty, muddy well (Jeremiah 38:1-6).

JOB.
The Old Testament book that tells the story of this righteous man's patient endurance was perhaps written earlier than any of the other books of the Bible. This fascinating piece of ancient literature gives us great insight into the way Satan works, the price of perseverance, and the power God possesses both to shape us and to bless us.

Imitators of God

One other thing: even when it's costly or inconvenient, be a person of your word.

Do you ever say:

- "I'll be there in half an hour"—and show up two hours later?
- "I'm not going to date that guy anymore"—but you do?
- "I'm committed to the student ministry"—and show up once a month?
- "I'll take out the garbage"—but you have to be reminded five times?
- "I'll get to my homework"—but you put it off and don't do it?

What if God waffled with His words? What if He said:

- "If you receive Christ, you'll have eternal life ... maybe."
- "I'll forgive your sins . . . maybe."
- "I'll be with you wherever you go . . . if I feel like it."
- "I love you . . . most of the time."

Those who are patient, who keep eternity in mind, are the only people who really live in truth—the truth of God's love, the certainty of His timing, the assurance that His higher ways are more trustworthy than our own. That's why one of the proofs of a patient lifestyle is someone who's committed to being truthful in the things they say.

If they tell you they'll be there, they'll be there.

Watch Your Language

This verse 12 also means we shouldn't feel the need to litter our language with cuss words in order to get people's attention or to give the impression that we're serious about what we're saying. A simple "yes" or "no" is always good enough when our hearts and motives are pure.

Part of the "judgment" James talks about is the one we saw in 3:1, where we mentioned Matthew 12:36: "People will have to account for every careless word they speak." But the more immediate "judgment" for being less than truthful is that sick, watching-your-back feeling that comes from covering your tracks and hoping you don't get caught in your own lies.

SWEARING.
In another flashback to Jesus' Sermon on the Mount (Matthew 5—7), James spoke out against the use of oaths—extra exclamation-point words we use as a way of indicating we're telling the truth ... honest! ... really! Both James and Jesus were proponents of "yes" and "no" simplicity (Matthew 5:37).

> What do you have the hardest time being truthful about?

5:13-18 Prayer Power

Anytime Is Prayer Time

There are two ways to look at verse 13.

First, whether we're "suffering" or "cheerful"—whether it's a bad day or a good day, whether people are being mean to us or treating us extra nice—prayer is always the right thing to do. The Bible teaches us to "pray constantly" (1 Thessalonians 5:17), which doesn't mean we're always supposed to be heads-bowed and eyes-closed but living all day in the reality of God's presence. Our relationship with Him never has to stop.

Second, prayer should not only be one of our responses but our *first* response to suffering. Instead of pouting or complaining or getting back at whoever's fault it is, hard times ought to send us into prayer. And so should the up-times. Rather than telling ourselves how great we are or taking credit for the good things God is doing, times of happiness are reasons for worship.

Praying for Healing

Another good reason to pray, of course, is when we're sick—or when someone we know is sick. For most of us, of course, being sick is usually as tame as getting the sniffles, running a temperature, or having a hard time keeping our food down. It's not that big of a deal. We just thank God it'll be over in a few days.

But we know sickness can sometimes become serious business, and James gives us a three-point plan for praying our way through it.

• *"Call for the elders."* Prayer is not just a private conversation between us and God. It should also be a

ELDERS.
These were men appointed to positions of spiritual leadership and oversight of local churches. Some believe the biblical titles of elder and bishop are interchangeable, making the elders equivalent to modern-day pastors and church staff. Others consider this a position to be filled by respected church members. Titus 1:6-9 as well as 1 Timothy 3:1-7 outline the qualifications for this office.

shared experience, where we expose our needs to other believers and ask them to go with us to God in prayer. This is one important reason for being part of a church body, a Christian community, so we can take our problems to people who care.

• *Be anointed with "oil."* In biblical times, oil was sometimes used as an ointment or medicine (like in the Good Samaritan story—Luke 10:34). But to apply it "in the name of the Lord" seems to mean much more than just mixing up an old home remedy. It's a symbolic reminder of God's presence, provision, and blessing. It's an act of obedience.

• *Pray the "prayer of faith."* As opposed to the kind of prayer James talked about in 4:3—when we "ask and don't receive" because all we really want is something for ourselves—"the prayer of faith will save the sick person." This is a prayer not only for someone to be made well but also to be "forgiven" and encouraged, assured of God's peace.

Verse 15. We all know people who prayed with deep buckets of faith, but they still didn't get any better and died a painful death. Why didn't God "save" them if they prayed like He told them to? Or was their faith just not up to par, not enough to get what they wanted from God? We sometimes say or think we don't have enough faith. We're not alone. Jesus' disciples asked Him to increase their faith. Jesus' response was that faith is faith. Faith as small as a mustard seed can move mountains (Matthew 17:20). It's not the quantity of faith. It's the object of faith! Having prayed, we leave the results with God who knows

OLIVE OIL.
Olive trees flourished in the Mediterranean environment, and most growers kept a press near their groves to crush the fruit and extract its yellow oil. Olive oil was used for many purposes—cooking, medicine, fueling lamps, and symbolic rituals.

ANOINT.
This is the practice of rubbing some kind of substance (usually oil) on a person's head or body for the purpose of healing or setting them apart for special service. Jesus' title of Christ describes Him as the "Anointed" One (Luke 4:18).

what is best for us in any situation. But think of it this way too: Is death the worst thing that can happen to a believer? Do you think Christians who've died in faith would trade their current living conditions for even a healthy body and a home in Hawaii? Yes, we should pray and ask for healing. But we must be content with God's all-perfect, all-wise, all-loving way of answering.

Verse 15. Another question that arises from this verse is whether or not a Christian should go to the doctor or simply pray his way to healing. Some groups do believe that it's sinful and faithless to depend on hospitals for help. But the Bible does actually speak about getting medical treatment (like in Luke 10:34), and we know that those who have been gifted with the abilities to research medicines and perform surgeries have been given their wisdom by God Himself. There is no less reason to give God glory if He heals us in a doctor's office or in our sleep.

A Spiritual Physical

Sickness is not necessarily the result of sin in a person's heart. But it can be. Even if it's not, periods of sickness are still ready-made times to slow down, to think back, to come clean with God, and deal with things we're usually too busy to think about.

Surely you've had an experience in your church, school, or family where someone you knew became really sick, or was hurt badly in a car wreck, or perhaps even died of a rare disease, or as the result of some freak accident. You remember how it made you sit upright, jarred you loose from the usual topics of conversation, and put your attention back on God and His grace.

It takes courage and humility to "confess [our] sins to one another." It also takes courage and humility to "pray for one another." But in these two acts of sacrifice—as we admit our own weakness and our dependence on the Father—He meets us with His strength.

That's one of the big reasons why "the intense prayer of the righteous is very powerful." It's not because *we're* so great, but because we've placed our trust in the only One who can meet our deepest needs. When we put our full weight down on the promises of God, He shows us again how true they really are.

SIN SICKNESS.
As a way of seeing how sin can sometimes lead to sickness, read Paul's startling conclusion about those who abused the Lord's Supper (1 Corinthians 11:28-30). But to be convinced that not all sickness is a direct consequence or punishment, read Jesus' answer to His disciples' question in John 9:1-3.

For Example

The reference in verses 17-18 to the fiery Old Testament prophet Elijah comes from 1 Kings 17–18. In response to the outright idolatry of King Ahab and his wicked Queen Jezebel, the Lord told Elijah to tell the king that he could expect several years of all-out drought in Israel.

Sure enough, the months rolled by, food and water became scarce, the ground grew parched, and prophets like the ones James talked about in verse 10 got to learn some real lessons in persecution and endurance.

But when God knew the time was right—three and a half long years later—He instructed Elijah to pray for the rain to start pouring (1 Kings 18:41-42). Miracle of miracles, the sky grew black, the wind picked up, and the dry spell was lifted by a heavy rain.

ELIJAH.
He was one of the most well-known of the Old Testament prophets, whose story covers several chapters from 1 Kings 17 through 2 Kings 2. He and John the Baptist (the one chosen by God to foretell the coming of Christ) were a lot alike—hard-nosed, thick-skinned—and were tied together by an interesting prophecy from Malachi 4:5-6.

Old Elijah wasn't perfect. "He was a man with a nature like ours." He could get scared and have his doubts (1 Kings 19:3-4). He could feel really sorry for himself and get tired of trying (1 Kings 19:10). Yet just like Elijah—when we pray "earnestly," depending on God for everything, He can make some amazing things start to happen . . . for His glory.

> Have you ever prayed about something, and even though it didn't turn out the way you'd hoped, you discovered later that it was really for the best? What did that do to your faith?
>
> _____
> _____
> _____
> _____
> _____

5:19-20 Back on Track

Not When, But If

Hey, this Christian life is a long way from being easy. With the Devil "prowling around like a roaring lion, looking for anyone he can devour" (1 Peter 5:8), and with our own hearts shaky enough at times to be "drawn away and enticed by [our] own evil desires" (1:14), there's a lot stacked against us. We have plenty of opportunities to "stray from the truth."

Still, we need to be sure to notice that there's an "if" in verse 19. We know we can't be perfect, of course.

But too many of us have set the bar pretty low on our obedience level. We half expect to lose a lot more than we win. We're not always willing to fight back very hard, to see sin as a trap to avoid at all costs. Failure to be faithful isn't the surprise it should be to us. Rather than evaluating our walk by reference to our often shifting standards, we need to take a fresh look at God's standards and His provisions for living up to His standards (Romans 12:1; Titus 1:8; 1 Peter 1:15-16; 2 Peter 3:11,14).

Yes, when we sin, we find forgiveness. When others sin, they should know that forgiveness is waiting for them in the eyes of their Christian friends. But our lives shouldn't be framed by the rationale that "nobody's perfect." We shouldn't want to be like everybody else, but rather strive to "be perfect, therefore, as your heavenly Father is perfect" (Matthew 5:48).

Run for Their Lives

We have come to the end of the book of James—a powerful, passionate appeal to holy living and humble trust. Even though he's pointed out a lot of troubles we can get ourselves into in the Christian life, he also makes it clear that one of our responsibilities as a church is to help people get back on track, to turn them "from the error of [their] way."

Understand this point: Our willingness to remain in close, everyday fellowship with God is not just so we can keep ourselves in a good mood. Our nearness to Christ and our love for other people can truly become a matter of "life" and "death" for others.

How much more fun it would be not to go along

ETERNAL SECURITY.
One of the church's hotly debated doctrines, which comes into play in verses 19-20, is whether a person who's a Christian can fall away from grace and lose his salvation. Jesus made it really clear that those who had received eternal life "will never perish—ever! No one will snatch them out of My hand" (John 10:28). The book of 1 John (especially 5:13) is also filled with passages on how we can "know" we have eternal life.

with a friend of yours who's stumbling into sin, not to excuse him for whatever he's doing, but to be one of the people God uses to rescue him, to pull him back from the brink of self-destruction.

James has shown us the way to be *Christian to the Core*—by submitting to God, resisting the Devil, cleansing our hands, and purifying our hearts (4:7-8). And every time we find the courage to lead someone into (or back into) a relationship with Christ, we get to play a real part in covering "a multitude of sins," in becoming agents of God's grace and salvation.

One Last Thing

There's no doubt that James hits us where it hurts. He convicts us of showing favoritism, of running our big mouths, of being more concerned about ourselves than about anybody else.

We might be tempted to come away from his little five-chapter book with the feeling that we can never measure up, that we're just inches away from stepping on God's last nerve, that the Judge who "stands at the door" (4:9) and sees into every corner of our hearts is going to prove impossible to please.

Yes, the standard is high, and God's judgment is sure. But what we need is not a lower standard of obedience or a God who's less serious about judging sin. We need a God whose Spirit can inspire us to live for Him. We need a God who is living proof that "mercy triumphs over judgment" (2:13). We need Him more than we need anything else.

James ends his book where we end ours—praising God that His truth will never change and being blown away that One so holy would choose to cover our "multitude of sins." It ought to make us humble. It ought to set us on fire and put us on a mission. It ought to make us want Him more and more. And more. And more. And more. And more.

> **?** Don't answer this question until you've flipped back through this book for a few minutes. What is the most important thing you learned on this trip through the book of James?

Notes:

If you liked "CHRISTIAN TO THE CORE" (Getting Deep in the Book of James) ...
Check out these other TruthQuest Commentaries:

UP CLOSE WITH JESUS
Getting Deep in the Book of Luke
ISBN 0-8054-2852-6

A LIFE AND DEATH EXPERIENCE
Getting Deep in the Book of Romans
ISBN 0-8054-2857-7

(available September 2004)

NEVER SAY DIE
Getting Deep in the Book of Revelation
ISBN 0-8054-2854-2

(available September 2004)